"Parental engagement is crucial for children's learning and development as it supports, encourages and nurtures them. Parents who are engaged in their children's education provide vital emotional and academic support which can boost their child's confidence and motivation, leading to better academic performance as well as better attendance and behaviour.

When parents are involved in their child's education, they are more likely to communicate with teachers and collaborate on how best to support their child's learning but it's not always easy to engage parents in the process.

This comprehensive and engaging book will give teachers and school leaders the roadmap for creating and strengthening the vital links between schools and families. It is bursting with positive actions and lots of practical suggestions building trust even within hard-to-reach communities."

Sue Atkins, *Parenting Broadcaster, Former Deputy Headteacher & Author of 'Parenting Made Easy – How to Raise Happy Children' (www.thesueatkins.com)*

"This book is an essential guide for colleagues who not only want to improve parental engagement in school but take it up a notch to empower families as a force for good in our communities. It's packed full of practical advice coming from the lived experiences of the author and contributors. Dip in, take tips and see what you can make possible in your schools to improve outcomes for all our children by unleashing the potential of family engagement."

David Whitehead, *CEO, Our Community Multi Academy Trust*

Building Brilliant Connections Between Families and Schools

This timely and accessible resource explores the complex relationship between school practice and parental engagement and is a result of rich collaboration between educational professionals, policy makers and innovators in bridging the often-challenging gap between school and home.

Considering the way schools liaise with parents and the wider school community, the authors provide ideas for innovative ways to develop relationships. Based on unique findings from highly-effective schools who are committed to bridging this gap, this book highlights the importance of using effective partnerships and practitioners understanding the importance of a transparent two-way approach. Case studies and first-hand experiences from educational professionals, parents and members of parent councils will reveal how school policy reform can positively impact school engagement and outcomes for children. This book covers a broad range of areas such as:

- Parent councils.
- Strengthening links between schools and educational settings.
- SEND – Comparisons between mainstream and SEN schools.
- The role of voluntary action groups within education.
- Fundraising and the impact of voluntary action within education.
- Building positive relationships that enhance teacher wellbeing.

Building Brilliant Connections Between Families and Schools is a key resource for all individuals interested in education, including educational professionals involved in academic outcome, community engagement and parental partnerships within schools. It will aid as a guide to developing approaches for teachers and school leaders, providing opportunities for growth within their own educational setting.

Jennifer Ross is a SENCO and Primary School Teacher, with a B.A. in Early Childhood studies and a Master's in Educational Leadership.

Building Brilliant Connections Between Families and Schools
Better Engagement with Education Communities

Jennifer Ross

LONDON AND NEW YORK

Designed cover image: © stilllifephotographer / Getty Images

First published 2024
by Routledge
4 Park Square, Milton Park, Abingdon, Oxon OX14 4RN

and by Routledge
605 Third Avenue, New York, NY 10158

Routledge is an imprint of the Taylor & Francis Group, an informa business

© 2024 Jennifer Ross

The right of Jennifer Ross to be identified as the author of this work has been asserted in accordance with sections 77 and 78 of the Copyright, Designs and Patents Act 1988.

All rights reserved. No part of this book may be reprinted or reproduced or utilised in any form or by any electronic, mechanical, or other means, now known or hereafter invented, including photocopying and recording, or in any information storage or retrieval system, without permission in writing from the publishers.

Trademark notice: Product or corporate names may be trademarks or registered trademarks, and are used only for identification and explanation without intent to infringe.

British Library Cataloguing-in-Publication Data
A catalogue record for this book is available from the British Library

Library of Congress Cataloging-in-Publication Data
Names: Ross, Jennifer, 1984- author.
Title: Building brilliant connections between families and schools : better engagement with education communities / Jennifer Ross.
Description: First edition. | New York : Routledge, 2024. | Includes bibliographical references and index.
Identifiers: LCCN 2023018146 (print) | LCCN 2023018147 (ebook) | ISBN 9781032115306 (hbk) | ISBN 9781032115313 (pbk) | ISBN 9781003220312 (ebk)
Subjects: LCSH: Home and school--United States. | Education--Parent participation--United States. | Parent-teacher relationships--United States. | School children--Family relationships--United States.
Classification: LCC LC225.3 .R67 2024 (print) | LCC LC225.3 (ebook) | DDC 371.19/20973--dc23/eng/20230614
LC record available at https://lccn.loc.gov/2023018146
LC ebook record available at https://lccn.loc.gov/2023018147

ISBN: 978-1-032-11530-6 (hbk)
ISBN: 978-1-032-11531-3 (pbk)
ISBN: 978-1-003-22031-2 (ebk)

DOI: 10.4324/9781003220312

Typeset in Galliard
by SPi Technologies India Pvt Ltd (Straive)

To my children – Brody, Jake and Rupert. Thank you for being my biggest inspiration.
In loving memory of my wonderful grandparents – John and Barbara Brown.

Contents

About the contributors	*x*
Foreword	*xi*
DR POOKY KNIGHTSMITH	
Preface	*xiii*
Note from the author	*xiv*
Acknowledgements	*xv*
List of abbreviations	*xvi*
Introduction	1
1 Parent Councils, policy and practise	5
2 Developing positive relationships and supporting mental wellbeing	24
KAREN DEMPSTER AND JUSTIN ROBBINS	
3 Strengthening links between schools and settings	46
4 Voluntary action	80
ALISON BODY	
5 Engaging the disengaged and overcoming barriers	94
6 Parental engagement: A comparison between mainstream and SEN schools	113
CATHERINE MCCLENAGHAN	
7 Reflections	131
Index	*134*

About the contributors

Jennifer Ross is a SENCO and Primary School Teacher, with a BA in Early Childhood studies and a Masters in Educational Leadership. Jennifer's additional experience includes; Parent Council Chair, Family Support Worker, Volunteer Manager and UK Sales Manager. In addition to speaking at key research and educational events, Jennifer has also contributed to a range of research and publications associated with parental engagement, including *The Mentally Healthy Schools Workbook* by Dr Pooky Knightsmith and *The Four Pillars of Parental Engagement* by Justin Robbins and Karen Dempster.

Alison Body is a Senior Lecturer in the School of Social Policy, Sociology and Social Research, and a member of the Centre of Philanthropy. Dr Body has extensive experience of working closely with voluntary sector organisations and has previously worked as a lead Commissioning Officer for early intervention services for Kent County Council. She has written numerous research reports and articles exploring philanthropy and the third sector, with particular relation to children and education. Publications include; 'Children's Charities in Crisis – Early Intervention and the State' (2020) and 'Engaging Children in Meaningful Charity: Opening-up the Spaces within which Children Learn to Give' (2020) *Children & Society*, 34(3), pp. 189-203 (with E. Lau and J. Josephidou).

Karen Dempster and **Justin Robbins** are directors of Fit2Communicate, UK. They have a wealth of knowledge and experience surrounding corporate, not-for-profit, internal and change-focussed communication. Publications include: *The Four Pillars of Parental Engagement'* and *How to Build Communication Success in Your School: A Guide for School Leaders*.

Catherine McClenaghan is a Primary School Teacher and Board Certified Behaviour Analyst. She has an Undergraduate degree in Psychology, a Masters in Applied Behaviour Analysis and a PGDE in Education and Leadership. Catherine has extensive experience of working with SEN children, and their families, in Abu Dhabi, America, Belfast and Australia.

Foreword

Dr Pooky Knightsmith

As parents, carers and educators, we dedicate our lives to doing what is best for the young humans in our care. We all want what is best for them and yet, sometimes, the relationship (or lack thereof) between home and school can get in the way of good decisions or positive actions. It can become rather 'us and them' and the people who suffer most are the children at the heart of these disputes or stalemates.

This book seeks to overcome that, at a time when our children most need the adults around them to work together to help to steer them through these unsettled and unpredictable times. Clear guidance is shared throughout on what has worked elsewhere and the steps you can take to replicate these ideas in your setting. This will enable and empower you to develop positive relationships between school and home and a culture of sharing and support that will benefit every child as well as creating a nurturing culture and ethos for those working with or caring for the children.

I have been interested in Jenny's work for several years – first triggered when she kindly wrote a case study for my *Mentally Healthy Schools Workbook* about her experience setting up and running a parent council. At the time, the work that Jenny was doing felt a little different from the norm,. Her council formed stronger, longer relationships with the school and became a more integral part of the school's strategies and processes than I'd seen happen elsewhere. I was intrigued to hear how it, and Jenny's work, would develop. Imagine my delight a few years later to learn about her book, that took those earlier ideas, approaches and ethos and considered what this could look like more holistically for schools, staff and parents of different phases, sizes, settings and types.

The book is a fantastically balanced tour through what the research tells us works, and what our colleagues on the ground tell us has worked for them. It offers very clear guidance, ideas and approaches that can be adapted for use by you and your colleagues in your setting.

Whilst every chapter was of great value, I was especially taken by Chapter 3, which explores strengthening links between education settings and home and does so through the voices of educators working across different phases and setting types who share what works for them and provide top tips for making it work for you too. Communication, collaboration and building a feeling of community shine through as the key ways forward in this chapter (and beyond) and there is real strength in the variety of voices and experiences returning to these key themes. As a reader, the range of different approaches taken and shared will inspire you and leave you with many, many ideas you'll want to take away and put into practice right away.

The book also acknowledges the times when relationships between home and school may be less positive, or lacking and encourages us to reflect on the causes for this – as educators, we are urged to be kind and remember that the parent or carer who presents us with the most challenge is likely the one most in need of care and support. I'd have to say that as a parent, this is so very true. Never underestimate the power of taking time to listen and show a little unconditional positive regard to a frazzled parent – it's really tough being a parent when your children are struggling with school, and it doesn't bring out the best in us; even those of us who teach this stuff for a living.

This book will be a valuable addition to your CPD library. It's not one to just read and file; read it and share it, discuss it, explore it. Pick it apart in discussions with your team and wonder 'What if?'. Revisit it as things change and move on. Most of all, use it to inspire you to set high expectations. Our children are more likely to flourish with a great team around them, with everyone pulling in the same direction. Dare to dream; then use the ideas in this book to make those dreams start to happen, one small, sustainable step at a time.

Preface

As a society, we seem to have grasped the powerful impact of communication, whether it is good or bad. If something goes wrong in the workplace – often the lack of good communication is to blame. So, if we understand the importance of it, whilst appreciating the challenges that are associated with it, why have many organisations and educational establishments failed to changed their approach throughout the years?

During my research and practice, I identified that many schools conduct what I would call 'maintenance communication'. This means the communication that they need in order to function on a day-to-day basis – the levels of communication that tick the 'basic' boxes; e.g. school dinner payments, school trips, nativity/school production notices, parents evening, sports day and PTFA events. Families are invited to participate, but under the structure of school and within the school's control. Families are invited, guided or directed – some may argue, this is a one-sided relationship regarding communication, being primarily on the school's own terms.

I wanted to test the narrative and see things from a different perspective. Imagine an equally balanced two-way relationship, where families were given just as much ownership and responsibility as the school. This opportunity with families could be transformational. However, how could this handing over of 'trust' and 'responsibility' be successfully implemented and managed to ensure successful outcomes for all?

This book is intended to provide you with the reassurance to both reflect on current practice and support you with the implementation of new strategies. This will be achieved through tried-and-tested ideologies from senior practitioners, parent council members, headteachers, teaching staff, education specialists and parents. It will also look at mental health, and the process of communication between settings and SEND, in addition to the wider responsibility of voluntary action in schools.

Representation matters, and this book will identify just how powerful the representation of all families in school can be, whether that be in terms of academic outcomes, mental health, philanthropic approaches or strengthened community engagement.

Note from the author

Throughout the book the term 'parents' is used. This term is used to describe anyone with parental responsibility for school-aged children.

This includes, and is not limited to: step-parents, single parents, nuclear families, grand-parents, foster parents, carers, legal guardians and extended families.

Acknowledgements

My sincere thanks and gratitude go to all the fantastic people that have kindly shared their time, experience and expertise.

Sue Atkins – Parenting Broadcaster, Speaker & Author of The Can Do Kid's Journal: Discover Your Confidence Superpower
Dr Alison Body – Director of Studies, MA Philanthropic Studies, Centre for Philanthropy, SSPSSR. University of Kent. Author
Lorna Clarke – Parent Council Chair, Basingstoke
Wendy Cobb – Senior Lecturer, Canterbury Christchurch University
Bethany Dempsey – Nursery SENCo
Karen Dempster – Co-Founder at Fit2Communicate, School Communication Expert, Author, Mum and photographer
Claire Frost – Head teacher, Kent
Lucy Griffiths – Primary Teacher and Wellbeing Lead
Dr Pooky Knightsmith – Author, Keynote Speaker, trainer and Director of Creative Education Ltd
Dr Emily Lau – Lecturer in Philanthropic Studies and Postdoctoral Associate, University of Kent.
Hannah Lee – Primary Teacher, St Nicholas Primary Academy School, Kent
Kerry Longman – Head of Year and Teacher, Marsh Academy
Nicki Man – Headteacher, Lydd Primary School
Dr Chris Martin – Honorary Research Fellow in Education, University of Wolverhampton
Catherine McClenaghan – Teacher, Board Certified Behaviour Analyst
Dave McPartlin – Head teacher, Flakefleet Primary School
Parentkind – National Education Charity Championing the Participation of Parents in Education
Emma Read – SENCo, Marsh Academy
Justin Robbins – Co-Founder at Fit2Communicate, School Communication Expert, Author and High Performance Coach.
Niomi Clyde Roberts – Assistant Headteacher, St George's Church Primary School
Kirsten Terry – Founder of Kent SEND Support
Alex Wallace – Content Producer for the Schools and Academy Show and former Teacher
Heather Woodcock – Inclusion Manager, Specialist Teacher, STLS.

Finally, a very special thank you to the parent council members and staff at St Nicholas Primary Church of England Academy.

Abbreviations

AAC	Augmentative Alternative Communication
ASD	Autism Spectrum Disorder
CPD	Continuing Personal Development
DBS	Disclosure and Barring Service
DfES	Department for Education and Science
DLA	Disability Living Allowance
EAL	English as an Additional Language
ECF	Early Career Framework
ECT	Early Career Teacher
EHCP	Education, health and care plan
EY	Early years
EYFS	Early Years Foundation Stage
EYPP	Early Years Pupil Premium
FLO	Family Liaison Officer
ICT	Information and Communication Technology
IEP	Individual Education Plans
NAHT	National Association of Head Teachers
Ofsted	Office for Standards in Education, Children's Services and Skills
OT	Occupational Therapist
PDA	Pathological Demand Avoidance
PEC	Picture Exchange Communication System
PEO	Provision Evaluation Officer
PGCE	Postgraduate Certificate in Education
POPA	Parents of Pupils Association
PTA	Parent and Teacher Association
PTFA	Parent, Teacher and Friends Association
QFT	Quality First Teaching
QTS	Qualified Teacher Status
SATS	Standard Assessment Tests
SEMH	Social, emotional and mental health
SEN	Special Educational Needs
SENCo	Special Educational Needs Coordinator
SEND	Special Educational Needs and Disabilities
SIAMS	Statutory Inspection of Anglican and Methodist Schools
SLP	Speech-Language Pathologists
SLT	Senior Leadership Team
TA	Teaching Assistant
UKS	Upper Key stage

Introduction

Communication is key, no matter who you are. Most of us have experienced good and bad communication at some point in our lives and can remember how these interactions made us feel. As I reflect on this from the perspective of both a mother and a Special Educational Needs Co-ordinator (SENCo), I experience and witness the impact of it first-hand. Every interaction leaves an imprint.

One of the biggest interactions in my life happened in 2012. I visited my local Children's Centre with my then 12-month-old and 3-year-old sons in tow. I attended, unaware of what to expect, and filled with a slight tinge of apprehension. I had only ever visited the Children's Centre for fleeting visits with the health visitor – a quick baby weigh-in and overall health check and we would be set on our way. However, once I engaged more with the facilities on offer, my knowledge (and subsequent personal direction) changed in such a way that the impact of this would reshape my life quite monumentally, both personally and professionally.

The welcome I received, and the opportunities that were presented to me, resulted in my professional career taking a swift change of direction with the offer of completing early years qualifications through an agency working within the children's centre. Having my own children was the biggest life-changing event to positively change my life. Although my values remained the same, I suddenly had a different filter – a new lens. I wanted my children – all children – to have the best experiences possible, with people that would care about them and help them to thrive. I saw a world of opportunities and gaps of potential development for families.

Now, 13 years later, one more son (three is the magic number!), an Undergraduate Degree, MA in Educational Leadership, a publishing career, SENCo qualification and a wonderful career as a Primary School Teacher and SENCo – I look back on those early conversations, encouraging words and Level 2 NVQs, and thank my stars that I walked into that building and was met with affirming communicative responses that guided me with encouragement and support. I realised the enormous importance of positive interactions with children and their families. As educational professionals we have a duty to work with families in such a way that we develop a partnership, one of respect and positive affirmation, to enable the best opportunities and support.

The aim of this book is to provide a number of examples that can be implemented within an educational setting, each helping to strengthen the future of our children. One of which is through my own lived experience, in the context of a successful parent council. This first-hand example will provide experienced examples of how parent councils can be achieved and the positive influential impact this group can have on the students and school

DOI: 10.4324/9781003220312-1

community that they serve. I believe that the most powerful tool we have is our voice; in this book, you will hear from parents, professionals and children about their own experiences.

My role as Parent Council Chair within a primary school enabled me to observe the relationships between families and the school. The council was a new initiative to help bridge the gap between the two. Following a successful interim stage, 22 parent representatives were recruited across the school within 14 classes, from Reception to Year 6.

Once the council had become established with this successful collaborative approach, we began to work closely with the needs of the children, families and school that reached far beyond our initial remit for the group. This included a deeper understanding about the patterns of disengagement and barriers to achieving successful connections and engagement.

As the success of the council became more widespread, interest began to generate from other schools and professionals, including Executive Headteachers and Ofsted Inspectors. Interestingly, what became apparent through feedback and conversations, were the school leaders that wanted the same experience, asking for meetings on how best to develop strategies to achieve the same success. However, all too often I heard the apprehension of change arise as the topic of 'allowing' permission for families to come into school was met with a multitude of concerns. This narrative highlighted the most significant element yet in the change for equal engagement within education – fear and the unknown. How can we progress if we do not let go of past practice?

Throughout the book, new perspectives will be challenged, and experienced practitioner perspectives measured. In addition to parent councils, we will also look at additional (and wonderfully unique ways) to build relationships with families and reduce barriers, ultimately positively impacting schools and communities.

The suggestions and recommendations within the book aim to provide strategies that will contribute towards improved collaborations between school and home. Clear conveyance to families and staff alike must be portrayed and understood within the school vision, informing how, equally, everyone plays a vital role in every child's educational experience. The term 'results' within this book runs far deeper than academic success – the aim is to support children and families in all aspects of their lives, helping to support the community as a whole.

The children will be watching, the children will be talking to their parents and friends, they will be influenced by what they see and how the world is around them – if that world is mainly the walls of their home and school, then we have a very grand duty of care and responsibility to uphold. They will see the importance of having a positive influence, recognising the impact of voluntary action and witnessing the power of the human voice. They are, after all, our future teachers, leaders and communities.

Chapter overview

Chapter 1

Parent councils, policy and practice – What does it mean? What is a parent council? How can you establish your own and what you need to do to make it a success?

This chapter will guide you through a tried-and-tested approach to provide the guidance for others wanting to establish their own parent council. The first-hand experience of teaching staff and parents provide insightful experiences into how parent councils run, and the benefits that can be experienced as a result. The chapter will reflect on the views of Ofsted and the success of St Nicholas's Parent Council.

Chapter 2

Developing positive relationships and supporting mental wellbeing – Karen and Justin look at the development of positive relationships and supporting mental health, including holistic and emotional investments that promote positive wellbeing throughout schools. This chapter will look at practical ways to build a healthy communication mindset and positive relationships.

Chapter 3

Strengthening links between schools and settings – A multi-agency approach is, without doubt, part of a school's very foundation for success. With this in mind, this chapter looks at the many different potential links between educational establishments and the way in which they communicate with each other. Establishments include: Nursery Settings, Primary Schools, Secondary, Special Educational Needs, Charitable Services, English as an Additional Language, home–school links, Leading during times of crisis, support teams and integral children's services. This chapter will identify how to strengthen links, share personal experiences and identify ways in which successful collaboration can be achieved.

Chapter 4

Voluntary action – Philanthropy within education has become an integral part of school functionality. Within this chapter, Dr Body identifies why it has become a fundamental part of education – 'Why do schools seek to attract voluntary action?' Dr Body seeks to consider the role of fundraising and voluntary action in education, identifying the potential pitfalls and possibilities from the lived experience of others and through literature and research from across philanthropic and education studies.

Chapter 5

Engaging the disengaged and overcoming barriers – This chapter will look at some of the challenges that schools face with regards to barriers to collaboration. It will uncover the complexity behind why these barriers are there in the first place and the challenges that they can present to schools and families. Personal reflections and lived experiences will be reflected upon throughout, in addition to suggestions on how to bridge the gap, identifying ways in which to build trust and how to develop strengthened relationships during times of challenge.

Chapter 6

Parental engagement - A comparison between mainstream and SEND schools – Within this chapter, Catherine shares her experience of working in mainstream and SEN schools in a variety of geographical settings: Northern Ireland, England, Boston, Australia and Abu Dhabi. This chapter provides reflective practice with regards to Special Educational

Needs (SEN), including what parental engagement means to parents and staff and the implications around communication, money, time, teacher training and Educational Health and Care Plans (EHCP) within SEN schools. Through the underpinning of research and personal reflections, contrasting practice will be identified and best practise explored.

Chapter 7

Reflections – The final chapter will review the key themes around parental collaboration, school initiatives, and relationships between schools and families.

1 Parent Councils, policy and practise

Parent Council

A council can be defined as follows:

1 An assembly of persons summoned or convened for consultation, deliberation or advice.
2 A body of persons specially designated or selected to act in an advisory, administrative or legislative capacity.

Where to start?

The first stage of change is often the hardest – either recognising that adjustment is necessary or simply deciding that an opportunity needs to be explored further, does not come without the prerequisite of support. It is without doubt that success stems from ardent colleagues that provide their full support and shared willingness to achieve. The modification of a policy or a shift in approach can often result in questions and the angst of the unknown. During conversations with headteachers that had seen the success of my own Parent Council and wanted to replicate it in their own setting, reoccurring concerns appeared along the lines of 'How will we work with parents in school equally and successfully, without impacting existing relationships?' Dialect then turned from excitement to apprehension – 'This will need careful planning', 'This will require careful management', 'I need to sell this to the team. I can see a few people feeling unsure about the whole thing' and 'I'm not sure what the governors are going to say about this'. As interest from visitors continued to grow, these common threads of concern began to replicate, time and time again. However, some individuals were determined to overcome these potential 'barriers', and continued their efforts to establish their own successful council.

Vision

As with any new project, a mission statement is essential. Creating this with a collective group develops a shared ownership and directive approach; have belief, have identity, have passion. Develop a group that will not only empower everyone within the school community but may also encourage other schools and education establishments to do the same thing.

First step nerves

Taking a step-by-step approach and creating a long-term plan, is the key to success – however that may look within your individual setting. Establishing a main goal, and communicating the wider vision at every stage, helps to keep your team and families engaged and develops a collaborative approach towards achieving objectives.

A 5-step vision plan of a school's current collaborative approach with parents is a useful structure to use:

1. Where are we now?
2. Where do we want to get to?
3. How will we achieve this?
4. How will we know when we are there?
5. How will we measure our success? (Mental wellbeing, academic results, improved community engagement, adapted school policies, reaching our hard-to-reach families.)

The potential opportunities for change, and the impact that a council can have, could prove to be monumental. The enormous potential for positive change is only as limited as those that are participating in its very existence. As with any new change or approach, the unknown can be met with equal amounts of excitement and trepidation. However, to strive for success, the main goal must remain at the forefront of everyone's mind and a consistently gentle recap over the group's vision will help to support this, particularly in the interim stages of the group.

What is a parent council?

A parent council is a collective group of parents that have a shared passion in wanting to assist the school in terms of improving outcomes for the children and school community.

Each class across the school would have one or two parent representatives. Their role is to feed information back to the parents in the class and take questions and suggestions forward to meetings – providing a 'go-between' for the families and the school. Council members can also raise their own suggestions, but these must remain for the benefit of the school community, not for personal gain.

In addition to the council members, there will also need to be a Chairperson, a note-taker and a member of staff from the school's Senior Leadership Team (SLT) in attendance. The Headteacher (or member of the SLT) would steer the group initially and be able to offer guidance and information. They will be there to maintain professionalism and direction for the group, answering any queries that may arise. During the infancy stages of a parent council, the Headteacher may be more involved in discussions, assisting with ideas and providing an insight in the school's current status. However, as the council develops, they may begin to provide a less active role within the group, offering advice or assistance, rather than steering the group from the helm. It would be at the discretion of the Headteacher to appoint a Chairperson for the group from those that have nominated themselves. This position would need to be filled by a parent, who would work in collaboration with the Headteacher and be the main point of contact for the other parent council representatives. This can be a very onerous role and will require an organised, professional and personable individual. It is a position that can be achieved through volunteer applications and an interview process.

Recruiting

A parent council needs members, and those members need to feel wanted, welcomed and valued. From experience, the more comfortable your council members feel, the more diverse your meetings will be, and the better the outcomes are likely to be. Each school and community varies, and each recruitment process will be just as diverse. However, what does remain a constant thread throughout, are the broad range of families and needs that they will have. Inviting parents to collaborate will generate a range of emotions, from those willing to accept the invitation with enthusiasm, to those who had feared school themselves as children and who still retain that feeling. No matter the situation, every family needs to be heard and needs to be reached – they all have an important role to play with regards to moving the school forward. Each and every viewpoint and perspective will play a part in securing a better future for the children within the school, whether that be directly as a council member or as a parent that shares a concern, question or suggestion with their council representative. The parent you may need as a critical element to achieving your success, may never actually set foot inside the school – and the vital link between council representative, parent and school can bridge this gap.

How does a parent council reach different families?

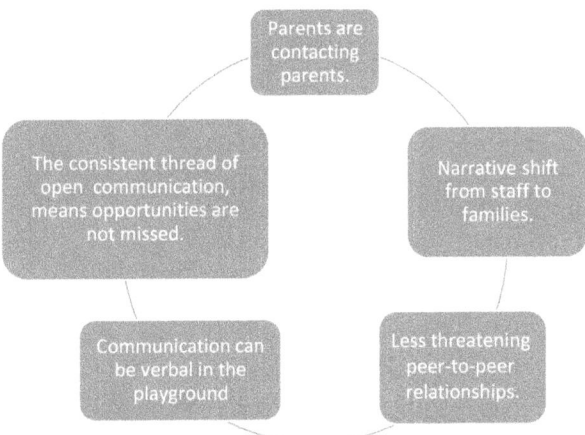

Figure 1.1 Image identifies the benefits and different ways that parent councils can reach families.

The passion for the group needs to filter through all avenues and every member of the school team needs to have the same passion and enthusiasm for it. Continuity is key to the process.

Why have a parent council?

Parent councils bridge, with the aim of closing, a gap previously left vacant between home and school. Good communication is a subjective topic, its success is governed by those that implement it, evaluate it and are directly or indirectly impacted by it. Whilst the proliferation of smart phones and devices have rapidly evolved the way in which schools can relay messages to families. The presence and involvement of families in school has developed at a much slower rate.

A parent council allows for a more personable approach for parents to work with and within the school, whilst peer-to-peer relationships are given the opportunity to develop continuously with the daily presence of council members on the playground. Whilst meetings are held at a dedicated time and with a focussed agenda. The opportunity for our more 'hard-to-reach' families to communicate on an ad hoc basis, allows for additional communication opportunities. Messages, ideas, concerns, questions and feedback can all be passed on through a third person, maintaining the amnesty of the individual should they wish.

The key difference here, compared to previously tried strategies, is that parents provide the integral part (or missing link) for schools to maintain a proactive approach. I recall an interesting conversation I once had with a parent: she compared the interlinking of families within a school community to rabbits in underground warrens. She continued to describe the family homes as rabbit warrens, with tunnels linking them to each other, whilst the school sat much more prominently on the surface, far removed from the hive of activity underneath them. It was the vital links (or families) underground, connecting with one another and sharing their difficulties, challenges or ideas, that the school really needed to hear and act upon. However, if narratives never reach the surface, how will change ever be achieved?

It was clear from our own experience that you should never ever underestimate the power of having just a few contacts above the surface; once they start to share the news, the gap will start to close, and the two worlds will draw closer. "Parental engagement requires active collaboration with parents and should be proactive rather than reactive. It should be sensitive to the circumstances of all families, recognise the contributions parents can make, and aim to empower parents" (DfE, Research Report, 2010).

This networking and establishment of parents within school requires mutual trust, respect and collaboration from all parties, with a deep explanation in the interim stages as to how this new approach may look and/or impact existing relationships. This level of trust between the school's SLT and the parents drives a specific and confident body. Collectively, they are there to work united to improve outcomes for the children and families within the school community, something which is proving increasingly necessary as primary schools face pressure at an alarming rate. "Unsurprisingly, schools and parents equally turn to voluntary action and co-production to help meet new challenges" (Body & Hogg, 2018).

In the section below Lorna Clarke shares her experience of setting up a new Parent Council prior to the Covid pandemic. Her reflection shares the successes and challenges she faced along the way – from initial set up to first meeting.

Lorna Clarke – Parent Council Chair

Our experience at the beginning was very positive with great enthusiasm from our Headteacher. He invited the local MP to the school to discuss the idea of the Parent Council (PC), getting her support and inviting her along to its launch which was also to be the launch of the school's revamped reading charter. According to the Head, she has some very useful contacts in the Department for Education (DfE) and is a good person to have on side when additional funding etc. would be needed. The local newspaper was also invited.

A letter was sent out to parents announcing the launch of the upcoming PC, inviting all interested parents to put their names forward for the position of class rep. The letter was accompanied by the PC's Terms of Reference as well as a document detailing the roles and responsibilities of the PC members. Aside from the parents who'd expressed their interest in becoming a member at the initial talk, one further parent expressed an interest as a result of this letter. I then met with the Head of School and both her deputies to go through the applications and decide on reps for each year group.

The launch was held on a Friday morning in January 2020. All PC members attended, as well as the local MP, the Headteacher, the Head of School, her deputies, the librarian, head of English, the new reading dog, the Chair of the Friends School Gazette and children from various classes etc. It went really well. I felt very positive about starting up the Parent Council. I felt that anything that could foster a sense of community, that could act as conduit and improve communication between parents and the school leadership would be a wonderful thing.

Parents have a tendency to talk among themselves about issues or gripes, with only the most confident or outspoken taking the initiative to bring suggestions or make their feelings directly known to the school. After hearing about the successes at St. Nicholas's, I thought that the Parent Council would be a wonderful opportunity for the parents to have a voice. The overall reaction of parents to the idea of a Parent Council was positive. Parents expressed that the idea of a PC was very attractive.

Things that worked well

The Head of School was very welcoming and accommodating. The school office created a Parent Council section on the website and plans were put in place for us to have our own notice board with our photos prominently displayed.

How were the first meetings?

They were all very positive. The first was really just for people to get to know each other, set our role and aims, discuss any urgent issues and agree how communication with parents would proceed going forwards. During subsequent meetings, with the Headteacher in attendance, there were questions e.g. regarding financial projects, that only he could answer. This demonstrated the need for a member of SLT to be in attendance, so that questions can be immediately answered.

Things that were more of a challenge

At our first meeting we agreed not to use Facebook or WhatsApp for communicating with parents. In hindsight, I feel it could've been a good idea for class reps to have WhatsApp or even email groups or similar with their individual year groups. It would have made communication so much easier, especially for parents who don't get to do school runs. Parents had to seek out the class rep in the school yard. It seemed grand at the time; in reality, however, it didn't work out so well. If each class rep had collected their parents' email addresses (from whichever parents were willing) they could have sent reminders about the upcoming meetings and invited suggestions,

> issues, questions to be put on the agenda. The Facebook group had been great for sending out reminders to parents (e.g upcoming Mufti days) so a similar thing for individual year groups would have worked well, I feel.
>
> COVID was a challenge! Our third meeting, scheduled for 16th March 2020, was cancelled and since then, aside from phone calls between myself and the Headteacher in September 2020, we have only had one virtual meeting on 12th October. COVID has caused cracks in systems and institutions around the globe and our little Parent Council was no exception.

Wider impact in school

The impact of a Parent Council can be felt throughout the whole-school team. Once established, parental understanding of the establishment and the reasoning behind school decisions, mixed with the ever-strengthening alignment of trust, can help to increase parental confidence and morale. The Manchester Transition project (Dyson et al., 2007), as featured within the DfE report (2010), identified a pattern of success throughout schools with high levels of accomplishment regarding parental collaborations, 'Good practice was found in schools which were proactive, had listened to parents, and refined their strategy to take account of their suggestions.'

What's in it for teachers?

Strengthening relationships, partnership working and the developing ideology of school systems and policies are the key attributes, and the very essence, of what the parent council strives for in its approach. By developing this level of understanding and working together to ensure the best possible policies are achieved, teachers benefit from strengthened relationships with their families. Additionally, a sense of shared collaborative responsibility and trust develops as a result of mutual collaboration.

The Parent Council at St Nicholas invited teachers to deliver sessions specific to their specialist subjects. By sharing advice, explaining the curriculum and how individual subjects are taught across the school and how homework supports children's learning in school, parents were able to develop a deeper appreciation with regards to wider strategic decisions.

Hannah Lee, from St Nicholas Primary School in Kent, shares her experience of collaborating with the parent council, sharing her passion for maths and developing parents' understanding of how the subject is taught and how this was received by an initially somewhat apprehensive audience.

> **Hannah Lee – Primary Teacher, UKS2 Lead and Mathematics Lead**
>
> **St Nicholas Primary School**
>
> Like any subject leader, I am passionate about my subject and recognised the potential that attending the parent council could bring. In comparison to reading, maths has always seemed to have a lower profile regarding a link between home and school, which almost seems to disappear entirely higher up the school. Attending the parent council meeting allowed me share how maths is taught at our school, and how very different this is to when parents were at school. There is often a lot of negativity concerning the subject, so

it also allowed me to gauge the parents' opinion of maths and ascertain our position as a school. It is considered normal for parents to listen to their children read or practise spellings; therefore, I believed a successful meeting would benefit the parents, teachers and ultimately have a positive impact for the children with their learning of mathematics.

I approached the meeting by explaining the key components to our maths curriculum, the learning journey and the thinking behind it. This enabled the parents to ask questions, gain an insight into how maths is taught and understand what a typical lesson looks like, thus allowing them to support their children. We also discussed the websites that the school subscribed to, which the children could use at home. Some of the parents expressed their concern of too much screen time, which was something that I had not considered to be a problem. This then triggered a review of our homework policy, something that the parent council became heavily involved in. It was important to take their views into consideration (as they would be supporting this at home), and they had some useful ideas. I am a firm believer that when people are involved in a process, they become more invested in the long run.

These meetings allowed me to get to know the parents better and to develop a professional relationship where they could share any ideas and concerns with me. With a representative in each class, the parent council became the ideal people to interact with other parents outside of the group, almost becoming a 'middleman' between the school and parents in a more informal manner. This, in turn, helped to build solid bridges between both parties and develop a team. I also believe that it set firm foundations for the remote learning that followed during the COVID-19 school closures.

The parent council has provided a good platform that we can build upon in the future; one where we can continue to investigate ways to support parents with their own understanding of maths and use this to support that of their children. One such way is through the use of Key Instant Recall Facts (KIRFs), which are shared with the parents on a termly basis. We are also looking to develop parent workshops where parents can develop skills alongside their children, for example manipulatives and how these can be used at home. This would become a part of the school's culture and develop alongside the child as he or she moves through the school. It is possible to do this with video clips from the internet or by using school staff, but I feel it will have more of an impact if parents are heavily involved.

Isn't it just a Parent, Teacher and Friends Association (PTFA)?

During the infant stages of the parent council, I was frequently asked: "Isn't it just like a PTFA [Parent, Teacher and Friends Association]?" Interestingly, this statement came from parents and educational professionals, who all struggled with the concept initially.

An initial hurdle appeared as people struggled with the concept of welcoming parents into the body of the school. It was almost as though the hierarchy of the school system was being rocked and many people could not understand why a new parent group was necessary or how it would work in practice. General consensus with staff felt confident with a PTFA, and Parent Governors had a clear and previously existing role, but a parent council presented itself with new ideology to overcome – both for the staff and the parents. It was imperative to have a clear narrative, explaining that the parent council is a different entity to a PTFA, whilst the emphasis on a collaborative approach for the benefit of the children maintains throughout both, the main duties vary considerably.

12 *Parent Councils, policy and practise*

Although the two groups operated separately, their strength grew when the two collaborated and support each other, this included recruiting members and understanding the need within the school – impacting on fundraising objectives.

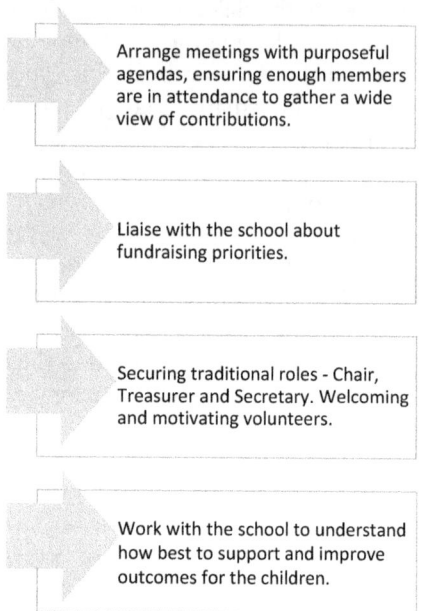

Figure 1.2 Circle of 5 suggestions showing some of the ways that the parent council can reach different families.

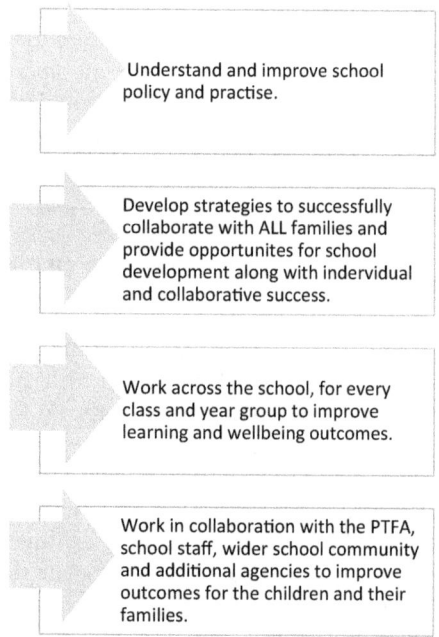

Figure 1.3 Eight boxes, with the key purpose and role between PTFAs and Parent Councils. There are four boxes for PTFAs and four boxes for Parent Councils.

Where to start

The Headteacher is key to the school's parent council success. Without the full support of the Headteacher and the SLT, the parent council will not establish the firm roots to develop, let alone thrive to grow.

During my time as Chairperson, I met many individuals working in schools who wanted the same success and asked how to achieve this. After explaining the fundamental logistics, many leaders would reply with, "Oh I couldn't trust our parents to come into the school and try to make changes". The body language of the individual changed almost instantly, from the intrigued to the uncomfortable.

The only headteachers that I met who had the foresight and confidence to develop their own council, were individuals confident in their own ability to see such a success work and who had the sheer drive to ensure that they were in this for the long run until the outcomes started to appear. Throughout the journey of the council, the headteacher (or subsequent senior leader) remained at the centre of the group, not necessarily taking centre stage, but steering the ship and keeping the team on track, providing answers and explanations when necessary and supplying their own suggestions to support the groups direction.

How do parent councils run?

The council consists of a group of parents that work to represent a class/year group/other parent. Parent councils vary slightly in structure, dependent on the type of school they represent. St Nicholas Primary School is a 2-form entry school with 14 classes in total and we had a total of over 20 representatives across the school. The Headteacher or Deputy Head will remain a key person at the core of the group. However, a Chairperson and secretary/administrator would be appointed by the most suitable methods possible, such as group or self-nomination within the council, supported by an interview by the Headteacher if deemed necessary. The Chairperson works in partnership with the Headteacher and will be the main contact for other council members between meetings. The week before the next council meeting, the head and chairperson meet to plan and discuss impending issues or topics for the meeting's agenda. The agenda is fluid, as subjects can be added during the meeting, dependent on any subject matter that are brought to the table from parents, via their parent council representative.

Clarity from the beginning

Once the headteacher and the SLT have agreed to the process, and have understood the aim of the parent council, they are fully invested in the process. The recruitment of council members is the next key point.

Establishing initial interest from parents starts with transparent communication around what the role entails, and the responsibilities associated to it.

It is very important that at the interim stage, it is explained to parents that, if successful, they will be representing their child's class. This is not an opportunity for individuals to come to meetings with personal agendas; they need to act as a representative for a wider audience.

Communication

Clear communication and a detailed explanation needs to be the first step in the process. It is one of the most important steps when establishing a council.

1 Use your newsletter, website and staff to tell families about the council.
2 Explain clearly what would be required of the volunteers.
3 Identify examples of the types of subjects that would be discussed, and which areas are not! (no private issues, only general topics).
4 Give the process time, the likelihood is that more members will join once the group is up and running.
5 Know your parents – Ask teachers to approach families that they feel would be good representative.

Highlight the benefits – Making a difference to your child's school and working in partnership with the teaching staff is a great personal achievement. Volunteering can be a powerful element on a CV and can help support parents returning to work.

Parent council role

It is important to vocalise the importance of the roles – they come with an element of duty and responsibility. However, what is paramount is to achieve a balance of recognising the responsibility without an overbearing narrative that will deter or alienate parents from applying altogether.

Parents are invited to apply, ideally through a variety of mediums, to reduce barriers to engagement and will have a clear explanation of the roles available, including chairperson and administrator, in addition to council members. It is good practice to explain that the roles of chairperson and administrator remain in place for a set time period, such as two years, and then others have the opportunity to apply for the role (unless individuals decide to step down before this time). This not only enables variety within the council, but it also supports as many individuals as possible with the development of their own skills and experience, supporting those wishing to return to work/develop new skills.

Professionals working within education, understand the importance of building trust and maintaining a sense of community – It is essential for these elements to filter through to the council. Fear and uncertainty create an atmosphere of anxiety and apprehension. Parents need to feel safe and able to voice their views to the rest of the group.

We found that moving the meetings from the hall to the staffroom had a positive impact on the group. The staffroom was more inviting and provided a more intimate environment. Psychologically, being invited into the 'staff area' sent a subconscious message to the parents that they are an integral part of the school team – it created one of the biggest culture shifts in the early stage of the group.

Managing volunteers

Managing any team requires compassion, excellent communication skills and a person-centred approach. Understanding each individual within your team and bringing together different personalities, skills and ideas can result in developing a wonderfully diverse and empowering group of individuals. However, this does not always come easy or without challenges.

Regularly bringing a shared element of interest to the group (linked to the council's vision) helps to maintain a strong sense of unity – no matter how unique members are as individuals, this is the common thread uniting everyone. Without every member, the council at St Nicholas Primary would not have achieved the success that it had. Maintaining momentum, and genuinely respecting individuals' contributions, is key to maintaining and developing success.

This level of management does come with a high level of work and is something for school leaders to be mindful of when recruiting a Chairperson. Applications and interviews for the position are crucial; they allow the opportunity to explain this commitment and identify how individuals will be supported in the role. Managing volunteers can be complex and time-consuming, a point in need of deep consideration by all when the early stages of a parent council are in discussion.

It is vital to remember that volunteers are offering their time for free – sounds obvious, doesn't it!? Each member is a volunteer and could leave at any time, so members need to want to be there and to feel a sense of achievement regarding their contribution. Council members are under no legal obligation to attend meetings, liaise with the school's families in the playground during their own time or respond to emails and WhatsApp messages; however, the success of the group depends on this. A careful balance is crucial, and each individual is different depending on their personal circumstance. Simple gestures go a long way. I always baked a cake and made sure to celebrate my members at any given opportunity. I thanked people regularly, even if only through a text message and took the time to invest in people's expertise and experience.

A large proportion of your volunteers may be working currently or have previous skills that can be used within the group. Within our council we had a member who worked in publishing; they offered to design and produce our marketing material. Her skills and kindness were invaluable to the group. The professional image and consistent branding helped sustain a competent and efficient image.

Celebrating

I was keen to celebrate our volunteers – without them, there would not have been a parent council at all. One of the ways in which we achieved this was through 'Volunteers' Week', which is an annual event held through The National Council for Voluntary Organisations (NCVO, 2021) and runs annually. We celebrated our volunteers during this time and asked all members to attend a special in-school celebration assembly. Certificates were presented to the parents by the local reverend in front of the whole school – this was a joyous occasion for the parents, children and staff and came as a wonderful surprise to all. Not only was there a shared sense of gratitude and appreciation, but the children witnessed the impact of their own parents' contribution to the school community. This created a powerful message of philanthropy for the next generation.

Conversations and opportunities

Many conversations that would otherwise have been directed towards school staff were now filtered by council members. Due to an increased understanding of the structure within the school, e.g. events and school protocols, we were able to answer basic questions on topics and advise accordingly – creating additional support to school and maintaining relationships between families and council members. In the case of questions and concerns beyond our responsibility or remit, these would always be directed back to the school. We became a quiet working force on the ground level and took pride in supporting the school team.

Many conversations were held in the local supermarket across the road – in fact, two new member recruitments were achieved in the cereal and cleaning product aisles respectively!

Whilst parents could register their interest to join the council either through the school office or by directly approaching the child's class teacher, we found that the majority of conversations took place on the playground or within the community with other parents (local coffee shops and toddler groups were also good areas for connections).

Policies

In the interests of transparency and equality, every council member received a copy of the 'Code of Conduct' upon joining the council. This document explains the roles, responsibilities, expectations, and the rules of confidentiality that will arise as being part of the council.

Having clear and sufficient policies approved by SLT and Governors is essential – it aids clarity and direction. This is imperative to ensure a clear roadmap for the day-to-day running of the group. By having a specific volunteer policy, it provided the school with a consistent approach to the involvement of the volunteers, along with the purposes of the group and the parameters within which they would be working. It also provided an opportunity to share the volunteers' roles, responsibilities and duties with others.

The policies provided a foundation for conversations at the beginning of the council's journey, especially when speaking to governors and SLTs.

Each council member received a document pack containing each policy, which included:

Code of conduct

Clarity of the rules and standard social norms from the offset is key to maintaining structure and transparency for every member of the council. It provided a basis of which to refer back to and can, during potential challenging circumstances, provide a platform to refer to the expectations and protocol set by the school.

Roles and responsibilities

The clear definition of responsibilities and the understanding of how each role plays an integral part to the council as a whole. The main purpose of this policy is to clarify, coordinate and secure standards. By providing clarity on each of the roles, each member understands the pivotal role that they play within the group and how they are interlinked to support each other. Having clear job descriptions helps when recruiting, particularly for the Chairperson role, which involves working in harmony with the school's ethos, Headteacher and the other council members. The importance and clarity of this role highlights the need for detailed job descriptions and suitable support from the Headteacher/Senior Leadership Team, should challenging circumstances arise and support from the SLT be required.

Confidentiality

The need for a confidentiality policy links to safeguarding, privacy and professional conduct. This can include reading information within the staffroom or overhearing conversations within the school environment. A precedence of clarity around the importance of confidentiality needs to be portrayed from the beginning, so that members understand exactly why this is so important and any actions that will be taken, should professional conduct be breached.

Volunteer policy

This provides clarity to every member as to how they will be supported, managed and welcomed into the school. It will identify expectations, protocols and responsibilities, in addition to the school's role in supporting them.

Parent council policy

This policy will identify the purpose of the group, linking back to the initial reason for establishment and the group's vision. It is very important to gather a collective momentum around the intended purpose and outcomes of the group.

A well-written policy will provide answers to three key questions:

1. What is the policy?
2. Why is the policy in place?
3. How will the policy be implemented?

School policies need to be clear and concise and should effectively communicate the subject matter to staff and parents. To achieve this, key points to consider include:

- Well-defined procedures.
- Potential outcomes/benefits to parents/volunteers.
- Potential outcomes/benefits to staff.
- Fair and equal opportunities.
- Clear language and simple terms.
- Consistency with regards to the language used so as to avoid confusion for the reader
- When using acronyms, provide the full term before using the acronym.
- Use present tense and an active voice where possible.

Policies that are readily available on school websites provide a transparent and open relationship with existing and prospective parents.

18 *Parent Councils, policy and practise*

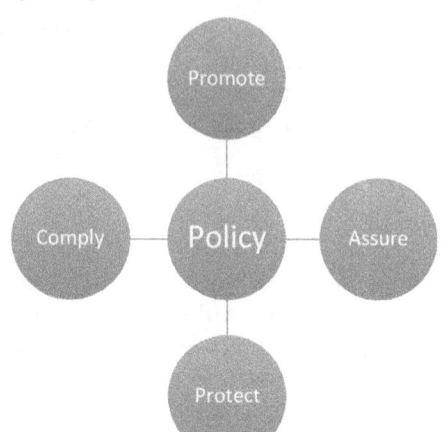

Figure 1.4 Central circle with the word 'Policy' in it; there are four circles coming off from the central one, each one with a different word; comply, promote, assure, protect.

What to discuss

It became apparent that early council meetings tended to start with similar themes – parking, homework, drop-off and pick-ups and fundraising events usually associated with the PTFA. It was only once these initial areas have been covered and council members began to learn more about the school, children, curriculum and community that the focus begin to shift.

Guest speakers presented on a variety of different topics and encouraged opportunities for different areas of discussions to take place around pedagogy, supporting families in need and local charities. However, every meeting was steered by conversations that members had previously with families on the playground, in 'casual' conversations. This is the critical element to add to every meeting, ensuring that the needs of those families that had previously felt unable to share their voice were heard and met. This element, mixed with a narrative from the school/speakers/topics, created a well-rounded balanced agenda, whilst developing understanding and generating broader awareness.

Building a brand and reputation within the school community

Planning and building your Parent Council is just part of a journey, and the development of a positive brand and reputation is a crucial step towards achieving success and expanding growth. Inviting organisations/companies and charities to attend the meetings helps to broaden the school's community approach and identifies possibilities of collaboration that, in turn, helps to support and enrich the school community. We developed our own logo, newsletter and notice board – adopting the professional approach that was identified by Ofsted, who met with us during their visit in 2019.

Projects

The first step is often the hardest. How will we make a difference? How can we make sure that this group positively impacts those in need? In addition to the main conversations that filter through from families and become part of the main structure of the council, schools can also look to improve identified areas of need through projects. By understanding your families and communities, you can better understand and support your children and school environments. By working together for a common goal, everyone can benefit.

Making a difference starts with the very first step, no matter how small. Start with the idea, start with a conversation, start with a vision. Making a difference can mean different things to different people. For one school, the main vision could be to ensure that no child starts the day hungry. For another, it could be to improve parental understanding of how maths is taught in school, or it may be to engage with the community more, establishing community projects and supporting vulnerable families through groups and organisations.

In our case we created an emergency breakfast scheme in conjunction with a local foodbank charity and began to establish links within the local community to meet the needs of our families, including a scheme to teach families about growing their own vegetables and how to cook healthy meals from scratch.

It's all about the children – Isn't it?

The beauty of the parent council is that you have representatives from across the whole school. This should include both new and more established parents. This diversity helps to bring a range of ideas and experience from many different perspectives. New parents can bring a fresh perspective and new direction, while existing parents have the opportunity to reflect on past practice and personal experience. The diversity of topics enables a broad opportunity for reflective practice.

Whilst the aim of the council is to improve outcomes for the children, it also looks to improve opportunities for families, staff and the wider community. The achievement of balance and 'success' within each of these areas is vitally interlinked.

School Council

The next step for the school was to develop a School Council for the pupils. The aim of the council was not only to listen to the voices of the children, but also to develop a sense of personal ownership and transformational change. After witnessing the success of the parent council and the Volunteer week celebration assembly, the hope was for the children to want to achieve a similar concept.

The process

After explaining what a student council is and what it does, the children then made the personal decision as to whether they would like to nominate themselves. This involved writing a personal statement about why they thought they would make a good representative. Similarly, to the Parent Council, each class would have 1 or 2 representatives. Should more than two children apply, a vote would be held.

> I wanted to be on the council because I wanted to help make some changes at school. It also sounded really fun, normally the teachers tell us what they would like, so I thought it would be good for us to share our own ideas. I was a little bit nervous about the first meeting, but once we were all in the room and the meeting started, I really enjoyed it. I had a list of things that my class wanted me to talk about, which included topics around breaktimes, homework and football.

> We all had our School Council badges to wear, so that everyone knew that we had been selected and that we were on the council. It felt really strange at first because the children were talking to the adults. It felt like the children were almost in charge and we all wanted to make things even better at school. It was a different experience and I enjoyed being able to share the ideas of my classmates.
>
> I hoped that we could make changes that would help everyone. That would be really good.
>
> St Nicholas Student Council Representative – Jacob (Age 9)

Collaborative approach

The impact of the Parent council became most prevalent once successful collaborations were established, both within school (through staff and student council) and within the wider school community. The meaning of teamwork became increasingly powerful and the sense of community strengthened through the outcomes made available to the children and their families. The school council identified how children from a young age can volunteer and identify areas to improve the school and outcomes for all. A recommended next step would be a collaboration between the parent council and the student council.

We all have a voice and a part to play in our children's future and education. The responsibility does not lay solely with the teacher, nor the parent. To create the best learning environments and maximum learning opportunities for our children, we all have a part to play, a duty to support and a responsibility to listen to the voices of the children.

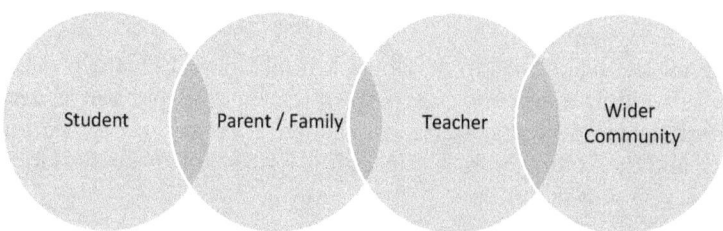

Figure 1.5 4 Circles overlapping, each circle holds a different word/phrase; student, Parent/Family, Teacher, Wider Community.

Connecting the dots – Listen to the need

During the infant stages of the council, issues were local and occasionally personal to individual families. As time progressed and clarity on the purpose of the group clarified and 'fine-tuned' towards collective outcomes, rather than individual ones, the discussions and topics of awareness changed significantly. As time and knowledge developed, so did the parent's awareness of the needs within the school and the variety of need within the community.

Some parents were unaware that a percentage of students come to school every day hungry, or of the level of deprivation that was so close to their own doorstep.

The key benefit to having parents as council members is that they talk to other parents. Sounds like an obvious statement, but the reality is that members were able to speak to families on an equal footing. This enabled issues to be discussed, that may otherwise have gone unnoticed.

We were able to achieve far deeper levels of support and understanding than we had ever anticipated at the beginning of our journey.

Awards and success

Creating a whole-school approach and a successful strategy with regard to working with families, engaging parents and improving outcomes for children was by no means an easy undertaking, but maintaining clarity on our direction was imperative – it had been our main vision after all.

Recognition for the school's achievements was not only a morale boost for council members, but also provided recognition and increased confidence within the wider school community. As a team, we recognised and celebrated our success within the school and team on a regular basis. However, recognition by Ofsted confirmed our accomplishment officially, endorsing the council's success.

During Ofsted's visit to St Nicholas, members of the parent council met with the lead inspector to discuss the outcomes that had been achieved, which were supported by accumulated documentation and evidence gathered from every council meeting:

- New successful group of 22+ parent volunteers across 14 classes.
- Newsletters, marketing logos and branding within the school.
- Interest from other organisations such as universities and various events, including: Presenting at the Sheffield VSSN (Voluntary Sector Studies Network) Event 'Small Groups, big issues? Researching local, community-based and "below the radar" organisations and action'.
- Presentation at Canterbury Christ Church University – 'Communities of Practise'.
- Survey sent to every family within St Nicholas School via Survey Monkey; vital feedback was received on how families felt the Family Council supported the families and school community.
- In July 2018, St Nicholas took part in their SIAMS inspection (Education Act, 2005). The new inspection graded the school as 'Good' with 'Outstanding' for its leadership and management.

Improved well-being amongst families that now felt that they had a voice within the school:

- "A proactive voice for the parents to enable change and direction in the school." – Survey Monkey
- "There is another avenue to put your concerns over if you don't feel you can go to the teacher." – Survey Monkey
- "Issues from the children and parents can be discussed and resolved in a safe, positive and diplomatic environment." – Survey Monkey

Ofsted

Reaching our families, and achieving positive outcomes for our school community, were areas closely monitored in relation to the Parent Council's success. To know that an idea, originally discussed on the school gate, which blossomed into a proactive platform for parents to become partners with the school, continues to be something that I am truly proud of. Whilst wider recognition was most certainly not at the centre of the group's outcomes, it was heart-warming when it did. As the hard work and dedicated approach came to fruition, we were recognised by other schools, universities, educational staff and professional establishments. However, as most schools will admit, there is nothing quite like the positive recognition of Ofsted.

> "The parent council offers significant support to help the school improve. As a result, there is a strong community atmosphere where parents really feel that their contributions are valued and acted upon."
>
> – St Nicholas CE Primary Academy (Ofsted, 2019)

> "Key to the school's improvement has been its engagement with parents. The parent council has been highly effective in supporting the school as it continues to improve. The school's vision of 'ambition, perseverance, respect, trust, friendship and community' is strongly supported by parents."
>
> – St Nicholas CE Primary Academy (Ofsted, 2019)

The statements by Ofsted identified officially, what we already knew – parents were engaged, we were reaching our 'hard-to-reach' families and we were rebuilding our community. The school received a 'Good with Outstanding Qualities' grade from Ofsted.

Ofsted (2022) identified that, in addition to key areas around education and curriculums, they are also looking at wider areas, many of which were discussed with the parent council. These include, but were not limited to: 'The personal development, behaviour, attitudes and welfare of pupils at school, the promotion of spiritual, moral, social and cultural development; and how well the school is led and managed' (Ofsted, 2022).

Through the extension of the council, and subsequently the children within the school council, we worked to develop strong foundations to empower parents and influence future generations.

Final reflection

"It's more than a group that meets every 6 weeks – It's the extensive arm that can finally hold the hands of the families we have always tried so hard to reach, but, as yet, had never quite made it." – Jenny Ross

References

Body, A. and Hogg, E. (2018). What mattered ten years on? Young people's reflections on their involvement with charitable youth participation project. *Journal of Youth Studies*. Accessed 7th February 2023. https://doi.org/10.1080/13676261/2018.1492101

DfE. (2010). Review of best practice in parental engagement. https://assets.publishing.service.gov.uk/government/uploads/system/uploads/attachment_data/file/182508/DFE-RR156.pdf

DfE Research Report. (2010). Review of best practice in parental engagement. Accessed 12th December 2022. https://assets.publishing.service.gov.uk/government/uploads/system/uploads/attachment_data/file/182508/DFE-RR156.pdf

Dyson, A. Beresford, E. and Splawnyk, E. (2007). *The Manchester Transition Project: Implications for the Development of Parental Involvement in Primary Schools.* Manchester, UK: DfES Publications.

Education Act. (2005). Accessed 10th October 2022. https://www.legislation.gov.uk/ukpga/2005/18/contents

Ofsted. (2019). Accessed 8th July 2022. https://reports.ofsted.gov.uk/provider/21/142814

Ofsted. (2022). https://assets.publishing.service.gov.uk/government/uploads/system/uploads/attachment_data/file/1099579/school_inspections_-_a_guide_for_parents.pdf

The National Council for Voluntary Organisations (NCVO). (2021). Accessed 7th February 2023. https://www.ncvo.org.uk/#/

2 Developing positive relationships and supporting mental wellbeing

Karen Dempster and Justin Robbins

Everything in education revolves around relationships – between teachers, the wider school team, parents, students and the local community. When we have positive relationships, we feel supported, valued and able to be at our best. But if those relationships are unhealthy, we can experience feelings of low self-esteem and confidence and reduced wellbeing. It makes our lives and work more difficult. Over time this erodes our mental and physical health, potentially to dangerous levels if the relationships become unhealthy, even toxic. This can happen in any organisation, and particularly when smaller teams are working under pressure together, which can often be the case in schools.

Let's get a little deeper into why relationships matter so much to our wellbeing. As human beings, we either seek connection or fear rejection. We can consider this based on Maslow's hierarchy of needs.

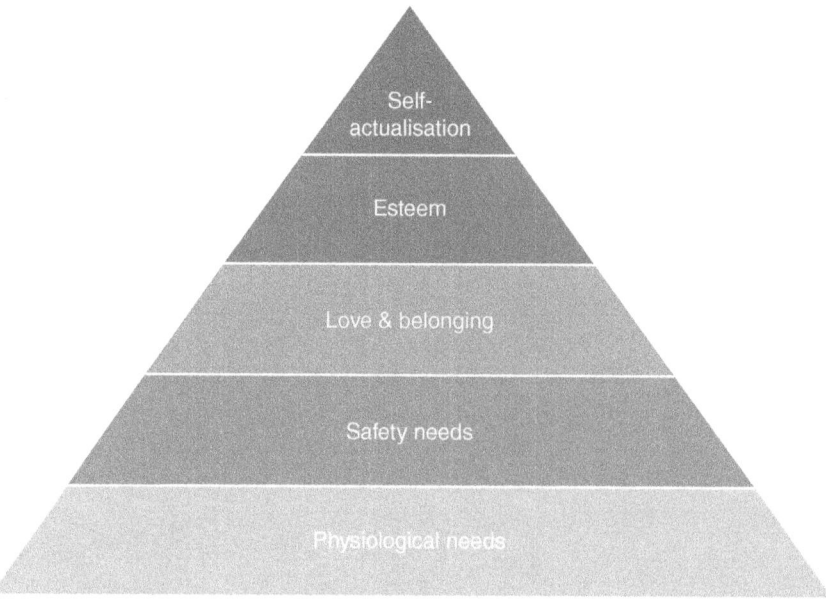

Figure 2.1 Pyramid of Maslow's hierarchy of needs. This image supports the fundamental elements required for enhanced wellbeing.

At each level we need connection, particularly when it comes to love and belonging. We need others to give us a sense of esteem and safety, however much we'd like to think we don't need the acceptance of others. Connection and positive relationships really are fundamental to our existence.

So, what can we do to ensure we have positive and healthy relationships when we work as part of school teams? Clearly, relationships are two-way in nature, and we cannot control everything. But we can develop the mindset, skills and knowledge to increase the chances of building trusted relationships, both at home and with our school team colleagues.

Now consider that at the heart of trusted relationships is communication. You may even have heard that 85% of our success is determined by our ability to communicate. We believe that the quality of our communication, and, as a result, our relationships, can help us to protect and improve our wellbeing. Many of us may think because we are born with a mouth and two ears, communication is easy, and we are all good communicators. But it takes the right mindset, skills and continuous learning (centred around listening) to be a good communicator – and that requires a regular investment in ourselves.

In this chapter, we share practical ways that teachers can communicate to build positive relationships with peers, parents and students that support wellbeing and resilience, for the long term.

What do we mean by teacher wellbeing?

Wellbeing is an area that has historically been confused with being happy. However, evidence and research have accompanied a mindset shift to prove that it is much more than that. Personal wellbeing is a combination of many areas of life, meaning it looks different for every person. In a comprehensive Gallup study of people in more than 150 countries, researchers identified five universal, interconnected elements that shape our lives: physical wellbeing, financial wellbeing, career wellbeing, social wellbeing and community wellbeing.

For teachers, like other professionals who work in highly pressured environments and to strict deadlines, wellbeing is more than a monthly coffee meeting or a weekly yoga session. It's about having a healthy balance between school and home, making time to manage the physical elements of wellbeing. Financial and career wellbeing of teachers are intertwined, especially as many who enter the teaching profession do so to make a difference rather than to make money, especially as research by the Institute for Fiscal Studies (IFS) (2023) found that teacher salary levels fell by 4–5% for new and less experienced teachers between 2007 and 2021. The price for being a teacher, at least during term time, can be a lack of time for self and other rewarding activities commonly associated with staying refreshed and energised.

In the 2021 Teacher Wellbeing Index, the most common signs of mental (emotional) health issues were insomnia, or difficulty sleeping. Staff reported a 7% increase in mental health issues in the past academic year. The three main work issues linked to symptoms of poor mental health were a lack of work–life balance, excessive workload and the COVID-19 pandemic.

Also consider that teachers are often taking on board a range of issues and mental load associated with individual students and families. They manage the effects of the education system and society on children's emotions and academic performance. However, unlike many counselling professions, they don't always have someone to support them, or it hasn't been seen as 'the done thing' for teachers to talk about such issues. The consequence of this build-up of constantly giving energy and time to other human beings is stress and an erosion of wellbeing, both mental and physical. And when teachers are stressed, this stress is passed onto their family, friends, colleagues and, of course, the students who they teach. Young people are quick to pick up on a stressed teacher and this creates an environment in the classroom that can quickly escalate into poor behaviour and reduced learning, putting even more stress on the teacher.

Research carried out by Leeds Beckett University and Teachwire.net in 2017 found that 94% of teachers' energy levels in the classroom dropped during periods of poor mental health, with many issues caused by excessive workload and constant work scrutiny. 67% of education professionals described themselves as 'stressed' in the 2018 Teacher Well-Being Index.

Ultimately, when teachers' wellbeing is diminished over a long period of time, they may feel that they have no option but to leave the profession, which clearly has a detrimental effect on students.

In her 2018 book *How to Survive in Teaching*, Emma Kell describes how disillusioned teachers are crumbling and leaving the profession due to workload, poor management practices, and long periods of negative stress.

It's critical that teachers have the full support of the school's senior leadership team (SLT), their peers and families to create a tight network of care and guidance so teachers can flourish and be at their best, despite difficult circumstances and workload. This must be underpinned by strong communication and a culture of trust, where there is 'psychological safety' for teachers to ask for help or open up about personal challenges, and the skills for peers and leaders to step in and support in the right way and at the right time. None of this can be left to chance. We must work hard to understand ourselves and how we prefer to communicate, how others prefer to communicate and then develop the skills to adapt our style to achieve the best outcome in any situation with different people.

What do we mean by positive relationships?

Imagine what positive relationships could look like in schools, for teachers. Generally, they will be built on strong mutual respect and trust. What are the ingredients that create trusted relationships which in turn support teacher wellbeing?

Let's start by considering what actions build trust generally. Look at the wheel of trust which is explained more fully later in the chapter.

These behaviours can be lived by individual teachers, to build positive relationships. It's important to consider that there are other factors that don't always make this quite so simple, which we'll look at in the next section.

What gets in the way of building positive relationships?

On an individual level, while we would probably love to have a connection with everyone that we have regular interaction with, whether at work or in our personal lives, we simply don't. This can be for a variety of reasons. For example, we may communicate differently to a fellow teacher; they may be overly talkative while we're essentially quiet. Or they may be driven by 'getting to the top' which may not be the same as our motivation, which are more focused on helping others. In such cases, we might say there's no 'chemistry', or we can sometimes talk in terms of a personality clash.

It also takes bravery to connect with other people. For example, when meeting a parent for the first time, who might be quiet and seems withdrawn, should you make the first move to connect? Many of us may fear rejection, whether a direct 'no' or a more subtle coldness in response. Our life experiences, such as assertions we heard our parents say when growing up, may have created an unconscious bias and closed-mindedness towards certain groups, or situations, resulting in us unconsciously avoiding or reaching out to establish a real connection. It could even feel like a transactional interaction, similar to tapping your phone when buying food at the supermarket, surrounded by strangers with whom we have no connection.

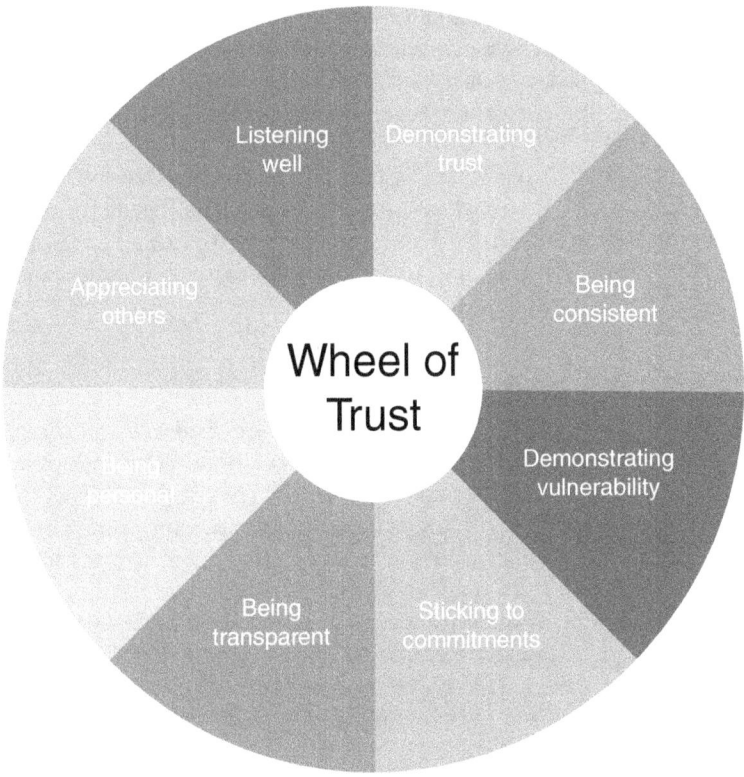

Figure 2.2 The image of the 'Wheel of Trust' is from the Roffey Park Institute. It is a circle with the words 'Wheel of Trust' in the centre. There are then 8 sections surrounding the central words, which demonstrate the eight areas linked to developing trusting relationships.

Over the years we each develop survival techniques and habits that may equip us to manage anxiety or deal with social situations that we find uncomfortable. For example, we might avoid speaking to a certain type of parent we find challenging or bury ourselves in our work when there is a challenging conversation to be had about their child. These can close us off, through unhelpful boundaries, to other people and may even make us seem distant and cold. As a result, others may 'give us space' or directly avoid a conversation with us.

It is much easier to build positive relationships in some school environments and cultures than others. For example, being transparent and able to speak up, and providing honest and constructive feedback, will be easier where there are high levels of trust across the school team. It requires leaders to shape an environment that feels safe, where teachers feel physically, emotionally, and psychologically safe at work, able to share details of mistakes they might have made or learnings they've had, knowing that the senior leadership team will see this through a supportive lens rather than one with 'consequences'.

In such an environment, leaders will encourage open dialogue and feedback (starting with themselves), appreciate different perspectives, help people to have uncomfortable discussions, support people to disagree respectfully, build the trust bank, show empathy, be inclusive and care and visibly take a stand for good. Activities such as learning walks are seen supportively with opportunities for real listening and learning, rather than as opportunities to find mistakes or make teachers feel like they are being judged. It's clear to see the positive benefits to teachers and students where such positive cultures are created and nurtured.

Sadly, there is a huge cost to teacher wellbeing where the culture does not support positive relationships. When toxic relationships are allowed to develop, there are imbalances in perceived 'power' and a lack of listening to teachers. Feedback is almost always taken negatively, and often personally. This results in repressed anger, resentment, damage to the school's reputation and teaching, reduced productivity and higher rates of sickness, unhappiness and teacher turnover.

Building positive relationships with other people

Now that we have defined positive relationships and recognised how important they are to our wellbeing, let's consider the diversity of people we build relationships with. We can develop approaches to build relationships in an inclusive way, where we all feel valued for our unique strengths and qualities. These are the foundations for positive relationships.

Have you ever been in a conversation when you felt your voice was not heard? Or a position where, even if you have managed to speak, the jargon used has made you feel confused or like an outsider. Perhaps the language used was insensitive to you because the person speaking did not demonstrate empathy. It's important that we develop the ability to put ourselves in other people's shoes. Often, this starts with us listening with empathy, to understand a little more about the other person, without judgement. Read on for ideas to help you to be an even better listener.

Words can be powerful. Words such as 'congratulations', 'success', 'exciting' or 'opportunity' can convey strong positive emotions. Similarly, poorly chosen words, such as 'failure', 'moody', 'impossible' or 'wrong', can damage relationships and hurt people. Being inclusive goes beyond looking at just protected characteristics, such as those listed below. While you should consider developing your understanding of the correct phrases and words related to these specific protected characteristics by contacting the right people and groups, you could also work towards using inclusive language on a more general level. Based on the Equality Act 2010, protected characteristics are:

- Age
- Disability
- Gender reassignment
- Marriage and civil partnership
- Pregnancy and maternity
- Race
- Religion or belief
- Sex
- Sexual orientation

To be inclusive with others who don't speak school language, such as parents, avoid using school or teacher jargon. Do not assume the other person understands what you're talking about. When you are speaking with parents and you use acronyms or short forms they don't understand, not only will they feel bemused, but they're also likely to disengage from the conversation. If you must use such language, take time to explain it in terms that others

We all communicate differently

Have you ever wondered why some people seem to do all of the talking and others don't seem to say a word? Or why some people seem to only care about hitting targets and achieving goals, while others are more interested in team harmony and maintaining relationships? In the ways that we each like to communicate, we are all diverse people as every one of us is different. We tend to communicate differently based on our behavioural and communication preferences.

Many of us have heard of introverts and extroverts, and some of you may even have heard about ambiverts, who are a mixture of both. These characteristics are often misunderstood and seen as shorthand expressions for being either shy or outgoing. While some introverts are naturally shy and some extroverts are more naturally outgoing, this isn't quite what is meant here. From a personality perspective, these terms are related to where we get our energy from and do not necessarily reflect how quiet or loud we are.

Introverts prefer to get their energy from within themselves. They will usually prefer to reflect when they receive new information, to ensure they have formulated their thinking and feelings before they respond. Think, for example, about the scientist who will pore through experiments and data, digesting the information, before taking a next step.

By contrast, extroverts get their energy from talking things out with other people and getting feedback verbally or through body language. Here, think about the entrepreneur, who loves to share their ideas with the world, tests them out in public and never seem phased.

Ambiverts can flex their style and exhibit characteristics of both introverts and extroverts. They sit somewhere in the middle. To a large extent, we are all somewhat ambiverts, at least from a personality perspective, as most of us have a mixture of both introversion and extroversion in our personality, even if one of them is just 5%. But there is usually a dominant type which tends to drive our day-to-day behaviours.

The psychologist William Moulton Marston created a personality profiling tool called Dominance, Influence, Steadiness and Conscientiousness (DISC), to understand the preferences for introversion and extroversion, and tasks and people. Simply speaking, people communicate based on four preferences, which are explained below. Once again, we are all a mixture of all of these, and they can be situation-dependent, but we each will have a stronger preference for one, or sometimes two, types. Which one do you believe is closest to you?

1 **Are you outspoken (extroverted) with a focus on getting things done (tasks)?** Do people sometimes consider you to be direct, blunt, decisive, competitive, assertive and often impatient? If so, you may have a red communication preference.
2 **Are you outspoken (extroverted) with a focus on relationships (people)?** Are you considered social, confident, optimistic, inspiring, collaborative and often emotional? You may have a yellow communication preference.
3 **Are you reflective (introverted) with a focus on relationships (people)?** Are you considered to be calm, co-operative, patient, good listeners, deliberate and often stubborn? You may have a green communication preference.
4 **Are you reflective (introverted) with a focus on getting things done (tasks)?** Are you considered to be independent, systematic, diplomatic, reflective and often detail-focused? You may have a blue communication preference.

Based on the way that we see and interact with the world, each DISC colour has a different filter through which we choose to communicate. If you have a focus on getting things done and are outspoken (red), then speaking with someone who is focused on relationships and reflective (green) could literally be like talking to someone in a different language as these two colours are considered to be complete opposites.

The good news, however, is there are lots of simple things you can do to spot preferences and adapt your style to communicate inclusively. It takes practice at first, but it's worth the effort to enhance your communication and relationships. Think about some of the parents you regularly meet, or colleagues you work with, and consider these tips.

Reds are goal-driven and like to lead from the front, so they will be direct and often impatient, using words such as 'when' and 'results'. You need to get to the point and allow them to take control or at least feel in control by leading the conversation.

Yellows are optimistic and able to see connections, so will be talkative and often not be good at listening. Their words will be 'who' and 'communication', so you need to give them time and space to be creative and be central to the discussion.

Moving across to the introverts, greens like to listen and feel safe, so will appreciate consideration and long-term thinking. Their words will be 'why' and 'relations', so allow them to think about wider friendship groups and try not to be too challenging.

Finally, blues are logical and detail-focused, so will need to see evidence and want rules to be followed. Their words will be 'how' and 'process', so be prepared with facts and allow them to demonstrate their expertise by listening to their clarifying questions.

Maybe with these tips, you've already started to think about which colour you might be, or even the colour preferences of those people who you work with or your family or friends. These tips might even help you to build better relationships with them!

After all, when we understand our own communication preferences, along with our strengths and blind spots, we can begin to form even more positive relationships based on increased self-awareness. Then when we understand the preferences of others and slightly adapt our approach to get the best from each interaction, our relationships can flourish!

Practical ways to build a healthy communication mindset and positive relationships

In this next section we will provide you with nine steps to help you enhance your wellbeing through positive relationships, with a focus on communication. These are:

Step 1: Start by developing a growth mindset
Step 2: Overcome anxiety or personal challenges when communicating with others
Step 3: Listen fully
Step 4: Manage difficult conversations
Step 5: Create safe spaces for positive conversations
Step 6: Lead positive conversations
Step 7: Build trust with different types of people
Step 8: Communicate positively under pressure
Step 9: Manage your personal energy

Step 1: Start by developing a growth mindset

Many of us may think we have a growth mindset – one that is open to learning. It's important to challenge ourselves to keep a growth mindset every single day and role model the continuous learning mindset we want so passionately from students. It's also critical to having positive relationships with parents and colleagues so we can learn from everyone we meet, avoid jumping to conclusions and have a more positive outlook on life.

Consider if you have an inner dialogue along the lines of:

- I'm either good at it, or I'm not.
- When I'm frustrated, I give up.
- I don't like to be challenged.
- When I fail, I feel no good.
- If you succeed, I feel threatened.
- My abilities determine everything.

Or if your inner conversation is more like this:

- I can learn anything I want to.
- When I'm frustrated, I persevere.
- I want to challenge myself.
- When I fail, I learn.
- If you succeed, I'm inspired.
- My effort and attitude determine everything.

The latter indicates a growth mindset. We often find that people who have this type of mindset see opportunities for constant growth and possibilities. They have a powerful passion for learning.

And even though we may have a growth mindset on the good days, we also need to maintain this on the difficult days when a negative inner dialogue can set in and potentially impact (negatively) those around us, either directly or indirectly.

A growth mindset requires us to seek out feedback wherever possible and take on board learning and insight so we can improve what we do for the future.

It requires us to believe in ourselves and have deeper self-awareness. We need to be curious to learn and redefine failure as an opportunity to learn. We have to move outside of our comfort zone and commit to our personal growth fully.

Questions to ask yourself regularly to maintain a growth mindset

- What made me think hard this week?
- What could I do/learn to better understand?
- Who can I ask for feedback and different perspectives from?
- What did I disagree with?
- What can I learn from this experience?
- What could I do to respond with a growth mindset next time?

Step 2: Overcome anxiety or personal challenges when communicating with others

Many of us have experienced that gut-wrenching panic of having to stand up or simply speak in front of others. It's one thing standing in front a group of students but this can often be a real challenge when we speak in front of peers, parents or others.

Fear of public speaking, or 'Glossophobia', affects three-quarters of all people and is frequently, but incorrectly cited as people's biggest fear. But why do so many people, even teachers who stand in front of a class of students all day, suddenly feel such fear when faced with a more 'public' forum?

Firstly, physiology kicks in – the good old 'fight or flight' response to what the brain might see as a potentially dangerous situation. That rush of adrenaline that leads to an increased heart rate, shortness of breath and sweaty palms as the body readies itself for battle. Or at least that would have been the response back in prehistoric times! This level of hyperarousal can be debilitating, which prevents people speaking in public effectively.

Then there is self-doubt ('I am not good enough') or a fear of failure which can also come from having a fixed mindset as discussed above. Add in a lack of experience in this area and it's quite easy to see why many people find such situations extremely challenging.

Here are some tips to help you to overcome your anxiety when communicating with others:

Understand how different people communicate – earlier in the chapter we talked about this topic. By understanding why people communicate in different ways to us, we can have a better understanding of their behaviour and we will be less likely to take it personally. For example, a parent who seems direct and almost aggressive may simply want clarity and succinct information to reassure them that action is being taken on their concern.

Breath and ground yourself – you may have come across techniques to help you to become 'present' and to move out of your anxious head. Consider the chair you are sitting in, feel where your hands are resting, think about where your feet are placed and breathe to calm your communication anxiety.

Prepare to be confident – we're all a lot more confident when we know what we are saying and have the facts. Take time to prepare for your conversation and be ready for the types of questions the other person may have. When appropriate, practice the conversation with a friendly school team member to help you feel even more confident.

Visualise – if you are a more visual person you may like to think about what you would like the situation to look like at the end of your communication experience. Simply close your eyes and consider what people are saying, doing and thinking, reinforcing your positive thinking.

Ultimately, practice is the key. The more we push ourselves to communicate and have positive experiences, the greater our confidence and the lower our anxiety.

Step 3: Listen fully

The average person talks at about 225 words per minute, but can listen at up to 500 words per minute. This means our minds are literally filling in those other 275 words to avoid being 'bored'. This explains why we so easily become distracted. Each of us has to make a conscious effort to actively listen to others.

Another reason is that we all have an ego – to a greater or lesser extent. We may enjoy being in the spotlight and at the centre of a conversation. In this case, talking feeds our ego. For these various reasons, we tend to listen more than we speak.

Below are some ideas to enable you to be a better listener. Give them a try; not only might you find that you can listen fully to what is being said but you might also benefit from others' knowledge and ideas and then make better decisions for yourself and others as a result!

Make your listening visible

Listen with your ears, body and face. Lean in, physically and mentally. Make eye contact, smile, nod and actually lean forwards, even if listening virtually. Don't let your attention wander around the room just because you are not physically in the same place as the person you're speaking with.

Make sure to avoid interrupting, no matter how strong your urge to do so. Not only is it disrespectful to the person you're speaking with, but it also conveys the attitude, whether you mean it or not, that what you have to say is more important than what they are saying.

Previously in this chapter, we shared the four different DISC colours and how these affect the ways in which people like to communicate. You should refer to the four different colour preferences and consider the following:

- Which DISC colours may struggle with demonstrating listening in terms of their expression?
- Which DISC colours may tend to interrupt?

It's important to adapt how we communicate in recognition of how others are likely to listen to achieve the best outcome. You should also think about how you might like to listen and facilitate that kind of environment too. For example, if you have a green DISC preference, you like to have time to think things through, prefer quieter environments and find sudden changes thrust upon you to be very disorientating. You might therefore like one-to-one or small group conversations, in less public areas and you may prefer to be given time to reflect on what you have heard before you respond.

Make sure you understand

Ask clarifying questions and share back your understanding of what you have heard to ensure that you understand what the other person is trying to communicate.

Start with some questions you can ask yourself to help you to understand the other person's story, without jumping to conclusions or judgements. For example:

- Do I fully understand what they are saying?
- What can I sense from their energy, body language and facial expressions?
- Am I showing them that I am listening?
- What could I ask to help me understand better?

And then consider questions that you could ask directly of the person you are listening to, so they know you are hearing what they are saying and are fully engaged to understand them.

- I heard you say … is that correct?
- Can you give me an example to help me to understand better?
- Can you tell me more about that?
- Can I do anything to help?

Generous and empathetic listening is an important part of Stephen Covey's Seven Habits of Highly Effective People – Seek first to understand, then to be understood.

We all listen through what might be called 'filters'. These have been built up through life-long experiences and can create bias, even unconsciously. We need to regularly reflect on our own thinking and question any potential bias. Lean into it and consider why you feel that way.

Learn each person's story

The successes, failures, joys, and sorrows that we experience in life weave together to form our 'story'. Our individual story influences the way we relate to others. When a leader or colleagues take time to understand the stories of others, they have a much better perspective and understanding of their motivations.

They are able to listen with empathy, putting themselves in the shoes of the other person, seeing the world through their eyes, understanding the filters through which they experience life.

Stay in the moment

It's easy to be distracted in conversations. You may be thinking about the next class you have to run to, the pressing deadline you're up against, or even what you need to pick up at the grocery store on the way home from work. While these are all important things to think about, they can distract you from truly being present and fully invested in the conversation.

Take notes to help you to focus and practice active listening by staying engaged. As a result, you will build trusted relationships with those around you as you'll make them feel valued by taking time to fully listen to them.

Listening virtually

The COVID-19 pandemic was a watershed moment for schools, accelerating technology needs and driving the building of relationships from a purely virtual standpoint.

While we are now coming out the other side of the overall need for distance learning, some practices that were started such as virtual parents' meetings have rightly continued in some schools.

To demonstrate we are listening in a virtual setting, it's important to have your camera on and to look directly into the camera. Avoid doing other things at the same time, even if it is reading something else on screen while 'listening'. You should give the other person your full attention as there is not really such a thing as 'multi-tasking' – we cannot usually do more than one task well at the same time.

When communicating through a screen, elements such as subtle body language, natural energy and even the tone in your voice are all lost, or at best filtered. While it might feel slightly 'false' or 'over the top', consider being more expressive and engaged to really demonstrate you are listening.

Here's a quick checklist to keep you on track:

- Did I chatter to myself in my head?
- Did I let the other person speak without interruption?
- Did I try to see things from the other person's point of view?
- Did I convey interest in what the other person was saying?

- Did I 'listen between the lines' to notice connotations and implicit meaning?
- Did I resist the temptation to jump in with judging comments?
- Was I honest? Did I show empathy?
- Did I treat the other person with respect, recognising their communication style?

Top tips to help different DISC colours to listen effectively

If you are communicating with someone who has a strong **RED** preference, they like to get to the point and understand how to get things done. Communicate with them in bite-sized chunks, giving outcome-focused points. They will probably ask pointed questions, so be prepared for these and don't waffle if you don't know the answer – just be honest. They will move on quickly so it's important to check they have fully understood your message.

On the other hand, someone with a strong **YELLOW** preference likes to talk! Unfortunately, this type isn't the best at listening as they tend to have a very short attention span. They are likely to interrupt regularly as ideas and chatter jump in and out of their head. Keep the conversation light, fun, and fast-paced. If you are presenting an idea or need their approval, then think about how to share in an engaging, probably visual way.

Those who have a strong **GREEN** preference are known for their listening skills, so lean into this. They like to reflect, especially on matters affecting them or others around them, so think about how to factor space and time in to do this. You might not receive much instant feedback from them but don't take this as a sign they aren't interested or haven't listened. It's simply a result of their reflective nature.

Of the four colour preferences, those with a strong **BLUE** preference are the most critical. They are also introverted and therefore make good listeners. However, they will likely ask lots of detailed questions as they process facts in their head. If there's a process or agenda related to your discussion be sure to follow it, otherwise you risk losing their attention from the start. Consider questions they might ask and make sure to give full details in response, supported with evidence as much as possible.

Step 4: Manage difficult conversations

Difficult conversations are part of daily life, whether these need to happen with students, parents or your school team colleagues. It's important to be able to focus on what's important while remaining calm.

In terms of parents, you are looking after what is most important to parents, their children. However well you communicate, there will always be situations where emotion overtakes logic or inflames an otherwise simple situation into something quite heated. This can result in a difficult conversation, which, dependent on how you respond, can either create a greater problem or ideally reassure and manage things to a positive outcome for all.

Consider the following to ensure you are ready for difficult conversations.

Put the date in your diary

Avoid putting off a difficult conversation for another day. Put a date in your diary (even if privately) to have the conversation and stick to your plan.

Prepare fully for the conversation

Gather facts and evidence before you start. Who do you need to speak with to gather background information? Consider how the four DISC preferences communicate when under pressure:

RED: direct and assertive

> They say what they want, expect immediate responses and appear very impatient. When your school team spot these characteristics, they need to be receptive and listen to the parents, get to the point quickly and be brief in their approach. They will benefit from offering suggestions and hints rather than directly taking control.

YELLOW: calm and friendly

> They talk openly around the concern but do not tackle it directly. They conceal their true feelings and only react when they feel challenged personally. With these people, it's important to be optimistic and positive. Have an open and friendly conversation and be ready for them to share their perspective.

GREEN: reflective and thoughtful

> They avoid conflict and worry about offending or upsetting others. Their drive is to find a compromise without harming relationships. Be patient, gentle and reassuring with these parents, giving them time to reach decisions. Make it clear that you value them and offer to help.

BLUE: reflective and questioning

> They appear to be efficient, rational and ask questions to explore all options. They ask for evidence and avoid conflict. Provide them with the detail they need and ensure your approach is logical and thorough. Give them clear and specific examples and work with them towards a potential solution.

Of course, your school team is approached by a diverse group of parents every day. It's not always possible to flex in the moment to everyone. But it will definitely help to keep these principles in mind for better relationships with parents

Structure your conversation with the GROW model

> GOALS: What would you like us to achieve for your child?
> REALITY: What is the current situation with your child?
> OPTIONS: What could we do together to achieve your goals?
> WILL: What will you do and what will school do?

Keep a positive mindset

Regardless of who you are preparing to speak with, keep in mind they may not remember what you say (exactly), but they will remember how you made them feel. Consider how you can create a positive experience, regardless of the message.

Confirm and follow up

When emotions are involved, facts can be confused. Confirm with the person what you agreed in your meeting and give them the opportunity to ask any further questions. Follow up agreed actions.

Step 5: Create safe spaces for positive conversations

Positive relationships require us to be able to challenge one another and share contrary opinions so we can benefit from different perspectives and ideas. We need to be able to say when something isn't right without fear of retribution. This requires teams that feel safe and where those around us have open minds, able to put aside pre-conceptions, biases and to listen fully.

According to David Rock, founder of the Neuro Leadership Institute, we rarely respond positively to what we consider to be negative or critical feedback – even if we have an open mind. Our brains have five times as much space devoted to dealing with threats (such as negative feedback) as they do to dealing with rewards. And anything that feels like blame may trigger our brains to react to the potential threat. As a result, we focus more on proving ourselves than we do in listening to feedback and different ideas to improve ourselves.

This is something to also consider as we challenge to ensure it is a positive experience that moves people forward and we are aware that different people prefer to be challenged in different ways.

Consider the following to ensure you create a safe space for positive challenge:

- Be a role model and actively encourage open dialogue
- Show others that you appreciate different perspectives
- Help people to have uncomfortable discussions – rather than avoiding them
- Support people to disagree respectfully
- Show empathy, be inclusive and care
- Visibly take a stand for good – referring to your school and personal values

If you invest the time in creating a safe space and listening with an open mind empathetically then it will build trust – and you will achieve more, faster with more engaged people. You will hear great ideas and you will benefit as a school.

Step 6: Lead positive conversations

As a schoolteacher or leader, you need to lead positive conversations every day. On any given day you might need to do so with your peers, other leaders, parents, students and many more. Depending on the person you are seeking to positively influence, and their personality, you might choose one of five different methods, as shown below.

Asserting – you would use this approach if you have a challenging personality, using facts and reasoning as well as demanding your ideas are heard.
Convincing – this approach works well for people who are more subtle, and prefer to use logic and reasoning to influence, putting forward ideas in a rational way.

Negotiating – this is often considered as a win or lose approach, but it should really be seen as a win–win approach. If you are happy to make compromises to achieve the best overall outcome this is the best approach.

Inspiring – leaders might use this approach, sharing inspirational stories to ensure the group as a whole feels good about the outcome and are enthused about the possibilities. With this approach you would communicate a shared sense of purpose.

Bridging – this is simply attempting to 'bridge the gap' with others by building relationships and making connections, often working in tandem with a negotiation style.

How to put these methods into action with different DISC colours

Applying the above to the four different personality types mentioned earlier, some clear influencing strategies emerge.

You might adopt a negotiation approach with a stubborn **red**, at least to get through any initial objections. Get to the point quickly and switch to a convincing approach once you have their attention, appealing to their competitive nature to get things done by presenting evidence and detail.

They might struggle to influence others due to their 'just do it' approach which can upset some people! Being task focused and to the point they might see others as simply an obstacle rather than someone to get on board.

Inspiration appeals to **yellows**, so optimism and positivity are compulsory! Keep the conversation friendly, allow them to share ideas or ask questions and avoid being too critical – especially of them personally. They are not keen on conflict so avoid any win – lose type negotiations.

This colour can have a hard time influencing others as they simply don't like upsetting people and then becoming unpopular or rejected.

A bridging approach, demonstrating lots of listening, works well with **greens**. You need to be patient and reassuring, giving them time to reach decisions. You might have to compromise and offer to help as their desire for people to be looked after will be strong.

The need to reflect can affect their ability to influence in the moment. Along with their desire to keep the peace and not upset anyone, they can find influencing others a big challenge.

Detail-focused **blues** need to be convinced with evidence. You need to meticulously prepare your facts in advance and give them time to go through these. They will ask lots of clarifying questions and will generally react badly to direct challenge.

For this colour to influence others, they need to believe they have all of the answers to any questions or challenges they might receive. Without this, they feel extremely vulnerable and are unlikely to believe in their ability to positively influence anyone else.

Step 7: Build trust with different types of people

Despite everyone being unique, there are generally two types of 'truster'. The first is someone who trusts implicitly until proven otherwise. They generally see the good in others and like to build trust from a positive standpoint. Some companies operate in this way too, where sellers start with a 100% positive rating and only reduce it when they do not keep their promises.

The second type of truster is much less trusting. For these people, trust must be earned, until past the tipping point upon which it is granted. Generally, these types are often more

Developing positive relationships and supporting mental wellbeing 39

cynical, maybe as a result of negative experiences of trust. Lots of companies operate in this way, where positive reviews boost ratings.

Let's look closer at the behaviours that create trusted relationships, based on the Wheel of Trust:

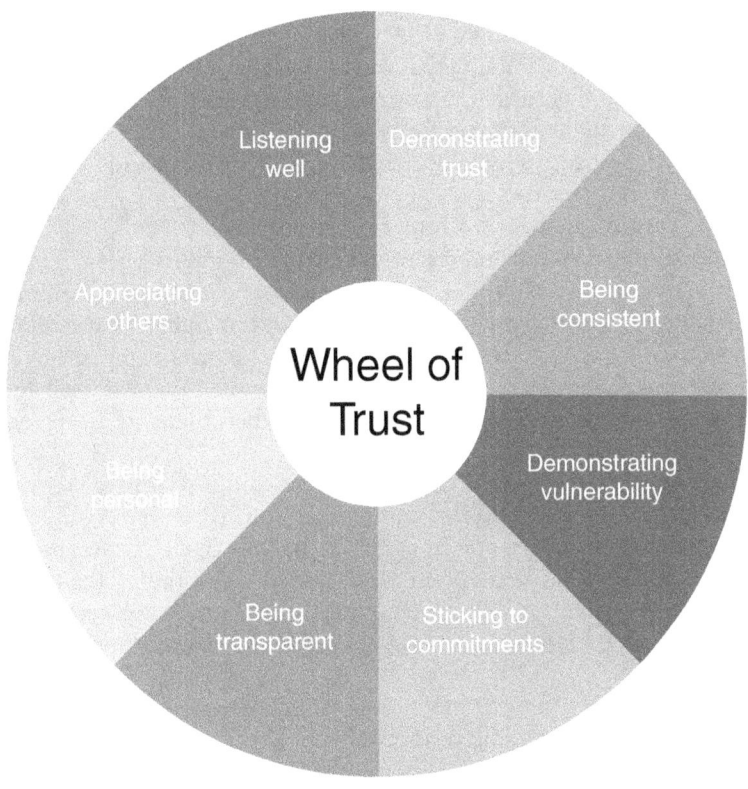

© 2016 Roffey Park Institute

Figure 2.3 Wheel of Trust from the Roffey Park Institute

Listen well: People are more likely to trust those around them who listen to their point of view and demonstrate through body language, responses and questions that they value their perspective. It's not enough to simply be present and physically listen to a parent or colleague. To build trust, we need to listen with empathy putting ourselves in someone else's shoes and opening our mind to new ideas and ways of thinking. Listening is an opportunity to show respect.

Demonstrate trust: Some of us tend to go into interactions with others naturally trusting the other person. We start from a position that everyone should be trusted, at least to a level. Others of us enter these moments with the opposite mindset and believe that trust must be earned. However, if we give a little trust to other person then they are more likely to trust us in return.

Be consistent: This is probably obvious, but we need to be consistent in what we say and how we behave, demonstrating trust in every interaction. This is particularly important when teaching in a classroom – students need absolute consistency. However, stress or difficult moments can mean we aren't as consistent as we would like. Afterall, we are all human and imperfect. If we can build a 'bank of trust' in the good times, then it makes it easier to manage the difficult times and when we might have a lapse of consistency.

Show vulnerability: By showing we are human and by being our authentic true selves, we will show a little vulnerability that will build trust with others. For example, when things don't go to plan, which can often happen in a school setting, we should take responsibility for our actions and focus on what happens next – to make things right or to repair any damage to rebuild trust, for example with parents, quickly. It is about owning up to your mistakes and imperfections.

Stick to your commitments: We simply need to do what we say we will, or we damage trust and create frustration and resentment. For example, it can be tempting to hear a parent's request and want to be the one to solve the problem by agreeing an action or providing a positive response. That parent will remember what has been said and will expect you to stick to the commitment. It's important to manage expectations clearly and ensure there is follow through on everything that has been agreed. Avoid trying to do too much all at once, particularly when there are so many competing educational priorities.

Be transparent: Transparency can mean different things to different people, but this is about having open and honest communication, wherever possible within your school governance framework. It is about having open conversations with colleagues and presenting them with your honest view rather than concealing or spinning information. By being open and honest we assure people that there is nothing to hide. Lack of transparency may give the impression that there is a hidden agenda.

Be personal: We all have personal boundaries and being personal is not about stepping over those. It is about building relationships beyond pure tasks. By sharing a little of what makes us tick, learning other people's story and being appropriately open about our views and concerns, we can be more supportive and empathetic of those in our school team and even with some parents.

Appreciate others: When we fully demonstrate that we appreciate the actions of other people, regardless of their status or power, we give them value and respect. We also reinforce that behaviour and encourage them to do it again. Importantly, we feel good about giving other people positive feedback. Consider when was the last time you gave a colleague or even a parent positive feedback about an action they took and how that made you feel or the positive outcome it had?

Step 8: Communicate positively under pressure

Stressful situations can occur in schools all the time. There's the unpleasant experience of having a conflict with a parent to having to deal with a full-blown school crisis such as a sudden school closures or unwanted negative media coverage that has parents at your school gates demanding answers. While it is not always possible to avoid some of these situations, the amount of stress they create and therefore their impact on wellbeing can be minimised through simple planned actions.

When a crisis happens

Managing communications during a crisis is about doing two things. Firstly, it's about ensuring that teachers and students are kept safe by having the right information given to them at the right time in the right way. This is what will traditionally be included in your crisis management process. Secondly, it is about managing the reputation of your school for the long term to maintain positive relationships. This is often not included in a crisis management process.

You can and should plan for the unexpected. You have regular fire drills to test the fire alarms and evacuation procedures. You should also have a plan that has been tested and is ready to go should a crisis strike, and you need to communicate quickly with your school team, parents, governors, the media or anyone else.

This should be a mini-communication timeline plan that allows you to quickly communicate with relevant people. If journalists are at your school gates or parents are gathering outside your office, you are likely to be too stressed to check the details and probably won't have time anyway.

Start by identifying the different types of crisis (or larger stress-inducing events) that might happen at your school and how they might impact your reputation and the wellbeing of your school team. Then consider who is likely to need to be informed if such events happen. Parents are always likely to be one audience, but the local community might be more interested in something like a flood where emergency vehicles are on site compared to a poor Ofsted report, for example.

Manage your reputation through a crisis

Having pre-prepared templates for messages that need to be sent out to parents, school team members or other key stakeholders is a simple, but effective way to both reduce the stress of a crisis and ensure you protect your school reputation. Messages written in haste under duress are unlikely to be as aligned to your usual way of communicating compared to less time starved messages.

Similarly, make sure it's easy to get the right information to the right people at the right time by having lists, key contacts or other logistical information stored in a secure but accessible location for when needed quickly.

During a crisis more than at any other time, what people say and to who will convey messages that may prove to be damaging to your school's reputation. To avoid such issues or school team members speaking to the wrong people, it is advisable to have in place simple communication principles for everyone to follow.

These principles should help to reduce stress and confusion by covering the following areas:

- Who speaks on behalf of the school? Who do they communicate with?
- Things to say and not to say e.g., avoid speculation, or specific names, etc
- How to manage people asking questions
- Social media guidelines

After the crisis

Depending on what happened, your school or school team may never be the same again. If you had an issue regarding child protection or a scathing Ofsted report, for example, it would take time and effort to rebuild trust in your school. The subsequent 'enquiry' is also likely to have an impact on the wellbeing of those involved so adopting some of the principles already discussed such as creating a safe space for conversations, listening, managing difficult conversations based on personalities are all crucial post crisis activities.

Step 9: Manage your personal energy

Most teachers are responsible for the precious children of 30 families. They need to invest energy in being consistent, self-aware, inspiring, empathetic, and, importantly, they also need to be able to protect their own energy, every day. But who helps them to do this, with long hours and regular emotionally charged moments? Often, this can be reliant on teachers creating their own boundaries, which can be supported through effective communication practices.

Below are some ideas to help you to manage your personal energy so you maintain and build your health and wellbeing.

Understand what energises you and what drains you

There are activities that have different impacts on our energy levels, and this will vary from person to person. If you know you need to do a draining activity, do it first thing in the morning when your physical energy levels may be higher. Also getting something done that you are less inclined to do means you can keep your day free for more energising and positive activities.

Be an energy radiator

There are people who we know who simply drain our energy when we are around them. It may because they are higher energy than us and we can find their presence overwhelming, or they may be rather negative, and this can also drain our positivity.

Consider the language you use, your mindset and how you use your energy with other people. By developing a positive mindset and behaviours, you will create energy for others. You are also likely to find this positive energy is returned by others.

Energise for the long term

It's important to be consistent in our behaviour and to have energy for the long term, not just in brief episodes. By pacing yourself and focusing on regular sleep, nutrition and other basic foundations for good health and wellbeing, you will be able to maintain your energy levels.

Set your personal boundaries

As mentioned above, you need to set your own boundaries to ensure you work, as much as possible, within given hours and have regular breaks to energise. While it is admirable to work extra hours, you can't be helpful to anyone if you don't look after your energy.

Be you

None of us intentionally try to be someone else at work, but consider if you are being your true self every day. If you need to 'act' and take on roles that are contrary to your natural preferences at work, you become drained of energy very quickly. You then need to rebuild this energy somehow – such as having some down time or alone time.

Consider if you are an introvert who has to act as an extravert at work. This will also be tiring.

Step 10: Build strong connections

Building connections with others is a great way to build positive relationships. Some of how this can be achieved has already been discussed in this chapter. However, for completeness here is a checklist of areas to consider when seeking to build strong connections with others.

Communicate with confidence

Be positive and concise. Speak at a good pace – fast-paced speaking can indicate nervousness which, in turn, leads to a lack of belief in what is being said. Take a deep breath, slow down and take your time.

Be aware of your body and what message it is conveying. Confidence is about much more than just your voice. Your body language says a lot too. Relax your shoulders, ease your jaw, stand tall, and take a deep breath. When you're ready, begin to speak.

Show empathy and kindness

Empathy is concerned with putting yourself into someone else's shoes and seeing the world from their perspective. We each have our own filter through which we see and experience the world which has been shaped by our unique background. Take time to ask questions and listen fully to truly understand how those filters shape someone's view of the world. This then allows you to show kindness without judgement, fully appreciating their position. It is a very clear way to reduce stressful relationships by reframing how you see a specific problem.

Be inclusive

When you understand the world from someone else's perspective you are able to be more inclusive of their views and needs. This in turn builds mutual trust. Often, you as the initiator might need to give trust in order to build it. This is especially the case when dealing with parents and students.

Be in the moment

One way we trip ourselves up when speaking is trying to conjure up what we're going to say next. Trust in yourself. Trust that the words will come. You can only say one thing at a time so stay present. A tip for doing this is to practice mindfulness.

Mindfulness means living in the moment and being self-aware. It can help to reduce stress and manage panic attacks, as well as enabling us to be happier and calmer in the ups and downs of life. Sometimes, thoughts about the past or future are all-consuming and detrimental to both our own personal wellbeing and our ability to notice those around us and build positive relationships with them. This can, in turn, enable you to just be yourself, reducing the stress of pretending to be someone or something that does not really exist. Looking after yourself and approaching challenges with self-compassion makes a great difference, especially as we are often so self-critical.

It is also about being present physically as well as mentally. It's much easier to build positive relationships in person so, where possible, meetings in person rather than virtually build a much deeper connection. Lots of unspoken information is lost when we communicate via email, phone, IM, or texting. The youngest generation at work, or those entering work during the pandemic, may not even recognize the importance of talking with co-workers in person.

Be curious

This means having an open mind. It means taking the time to learn someone's story or their motives. If you find yourself (and that little voice in your head) arguing, prepping your response, or refuting what your colleague is saying, you are not focused on thoroughly understanding their communication. You have stopped being curious and have refocused the discussion on your needs.

At the same time look for nonverbal communication - it is a powerful voice in any interaction. The voice tonality, body language, and facial expressions speak more loudly than verbal communication or the actual words in many communication exchanges.

In any communication, the opportunity for misunderstanding is ever present. Look for patterns ('Is this how this person usually reacts?') and inconsistencies ('Is this consistent with what I expect from this person?').

If any of these verbal and nonverbal communication factors are inconsistent or sending different messages, it's likely going to lead to a conflict or stressful situation.

Consider what might work rather than what will fail. Think about the possibility rather than the impossibilities. A great way to build positive relationships is to always listen for opportunities and seek to make them happen. We can often have things in common that we didn't know about.

Connections everywhere

Here is an example of building a connection when perhaps there seemed liked nothing existed. In a school in America, a teacher and students were asked to write down answers to some questions about themselves, such as their favourite sports teams or favourite food dishes. They did so and exchanged answers with each other. As they did, they realised that many of them had more in common than they had originally thought, breaking down barriers and supporting students in being at their best.

Conclusion

Positive relationships within a school have a huge impact on the wellbeing of the school team, students, their families and even the wider community. The first foundation in building any relationship is communication, which itself has many facets. From speaking with confidence, managing difficult conversations, listening and ultimately building trust – none of these will happen by chance; they must all be systematically and deliberately developed.

The key here is having a long-term plan, one which starts with the foundation of healthy relationships built on mutual trust and understanding. Skills can be learned, and training can be given, but they need the backdrop of a planned approach to building positive relationships through inclusive communication.

References

Equality Act. (2010). Accessed 27th September 2022. https://www.legislation.gov.uk/ukpga/2010/15/contents

Institute for Fiscal Studies. (2023). The even longer squeeze on teacher pay. Accessed 10th January 2023. https://ifs.org.uk/articles/even-longer-squeeze-teacher-pay The even longer squeeze on teacher pay | Institute for Fiscal Studies (ifs.org.uk)

Kell, E. (2018). *How to Survive in Education*. London: Bloomsbury.

Teacher Wellbeing Index. (2021). Accessed 11th November 2022. https://www.educationsupport.org.uk/media/qzna4gxb/twix-2021.pdf

3 Strengthening links between schools and settings

Introduction

Teamwork – A word we use on a frequent basis within the classroom. School staff often use the word to demonstrate the importance of collaboration, whilst identifying the power of working together to achieve a common goal.

So, I have to ask the question – Why do we, as adults, who encourage teamwork within our school walls, struggle to achieve this wholeheartedly and without faltering when working with external settings and professionals?

In addition to reflecting on research and pedagogical approaches, industry professionals share their experiences and top tips with regards to developing and nurturing professional relationships.

Collaborate – communicate – community

Often when we reflect on our own communication methods, we analyse how we communicate and review what is and isn't working well. However, successful collaboration and communication, terms and words that can be used so flippantly, is not always achieved with the necessary balance and sustainability required for the desired favourable outcomes.

Objectives and outcomes require a focus – a central point from which to reflect from and keep at the heart of the very purpose of why you are communicating with others in the first instance.

The central piece of the puzzle, of course, remains the children. The Children's Act of 2004 did exactly that when it placed the child at the centre of the community. As children, our experiences within school and the relationships with the professionals we interact with, help to shape us as individuals. Positive experiences lead to increased engagement and improved outcomes (Goodall, 2017).

Community and communication – two areas that we know need to run deep with passion and excellence. We look to build firm foundations upon which to build the community of hope, education, security, guidance and respect. With the children in our care, at the heart of everything we do, are we maximising opportunities to make the school years as effective as possible?

This begs the questions – Are we doing enough? How can we improve? Is our blueprint bulletproof, or do we need to revisit the drawing board? How can our policies work in harmony with other schools and settings if we are all working to our own personal agendas and systems?

The potential for developing communication is not to be restricted to one establishment, whether that be the one within which you currently work, or a collaboration with another school of professional body.

Within education, the constant overlay of professional interactions and relationships is clearly apparent, as the needs of the children and families must be met. However, it has become apparent that the system is full of obvious cracks and empty opportunities for improvement.

Whilst inter-settings and school collaborations can be complex, there are a wide range of collaborative activities that can smooth transition and improve outcomes for children. Varying circumstances and individual relationships can provide differing outcomes. Dr Paul Armstrong (DfE, 2015a) identified that despite an increase in inter-school activity since 2000, knowledge remains limited in this area, as does its effect in terms of student outcomes.

Whilst some may argue that it can prove more difficult to manage multiple relationships, my response would be that it provides the opportunity to close the gap faster – the more professional links, the better! It only makes for wider possibilities and prospects – we just need to have the conversations and begin to pave the way for change and success.

The link between home and school

Regardless of a child's age or stage of education, the link between home and school is a vital part to collaborative success:

> It is important to note that this means that the remit of the school leader extends beyond the school gates, just as learning extends well beyond the confines of the school; schooling is a subset of education, which is itself a subset of the much larger process of learning.
> (Goodall, 2017)

After years of research, Parentkind created a Blueprint for parent-friendly schools and effective two-way communication was highlighted as the key to achieving successful outcomes for families, children and schools.

Understanding the impact and importance of positive relationships between schools and settings is a great base to work from. Parentkind share their own reflection and 'Top Ten Tips' to achieving this.

Parentkind

The relationship between home and school works best when it's close, productive and open-minded. Too many of us have been in situations where it feels as if your child's school is only in touch when things have gone wrong, or when they have bad news to tell you.

Many parents don't feel listened to and they face too many barriers: feeling that they don't have the time, not being asked and not knowing what skills and knowledge they can offer.

Teachers tell us that they know there are benefits to parental participation and that it improves outcomes for young people. But they also tell us they don't feel confident in dealing with parents and most schools don't have a parent engagement lead, or a written plan.

To address this situation, Parentkind created its Blueprint for Parent-Friendly Schools. This plan, which can be used in any educational setting, was put together with the help of Canterbury Christ Church University. It has a clear focus: reinforcing success in parental participation in schools.

Through the years of work and research that culminated in the Blueprint, it became clear that effective two-way communication is absolutely paramount. Parents are clear that when schools broadcast information but don't listen or engage in conversation, the relationship starts to suffer and benefits to young people begin to be lost.

Parentkind's top tips:

1 Ask parents. Use surveys and feedback forms to engage parents in two-way conversation. It's incredibly important to get a regular snapshot of their views and to ensure parents feel heard.
2 Increase the use of technology. Use tools and platforms online to streamline and support communication. This decreases the paper trail and means that parents can participate from a place of their choosing where they're comfortable.
3 Translate things into different languages. To ensure a shared understanding, all parents need to be able to access information. Translating communications into different languages can be especially helpful.

Parentkind piloted its Blueprint for Parent-Friendly Schools at a secondary school in Doncaster. At this school, only 48 parents engaged with Ofsted's 'Parent View', despite it catering for over 1200 students. There were parent governors, but they weren't entirely representative of the school's intake or of the views of its parent community.

To tackle this, a Parent Council was set up – a new, accessible and non-threatening way for parents to participate in the life of the school. When the idea was promoted with a survey, 243 parents responded and gave their views.

This example goes to show: to get this right, no idea is off-limits. For some schools, a Parent Council might be the answer; for others, a truly engaged parent population might be achieved by regular surveys, online snap-polls and 'You said, we did'-type communications. The key thing is that parents feel listened to and that they know their views have made a difference.

Kerry-Jane Packman

Executive Director, Parentkind

Parentkind is a national charity that gives those with a parenting role a voice in education. It is home to a network of around 13,000 PTA fundraisers that raise over £120 million per year.

www.parentkind.org.uk

Collaboration for all-Inclusive practice

When discussing inclusive practice and collaboration for all, it is easy to forget the many different schools, services and professionals that are included in this remit. Educational professionals understand the complexity of multi-agency working. Depending on the needs of the child/family and the child's age, these professionals could include (but are not limited to);

- Nurseries
- Pre-Schools
- Primary Schools
- Secondary Schools
- SEND Provisions
- Behavioural and Support Teams
- Children and Adolescent Mental Health Service (CAMHS)
- Occupational Therapy Service
- Speech and Language Therapy Service
- SEN Support Team
- Education Psychology Service
- Integrated Children's Service
- School Nurse

> I was new to the role and, at times, was overwhelmed by the many different health care professionals, therapists, speech and language consultants, specialist teaching services and numerous other professionals associated with our children who worked to meet the child's specific needs. I was positively humbled by the broad range of people working tirelessly to support our children and families, yet felt a huge responsibility to ensure the communication and success was met as a central point of contact for all.
>
> Anonymous – SENCO

Understanding how every agency works and how to 'get the best' out of every service, every meeting and every situation can be a daunting prospect. Research by Chris James (2007) looked at disadvantaged primary schools in Wales where, against all the odds, students reached very high levels of attainment.

The features within the report included, 'leadership; the mindset; the teaching team; the engagement and commitment of the pupils and their parents; very efficient and effective organisation and management; and mutual support, validation and valuing from all those connected with the school'. The undeniable focus and importance on good collaborative practice within the report highlighted the positive impact that can be achieved, regardless of social or economic status.

Heather Woodcock, Inclusion Manager, shares her experience of successful collaborative working and the valuable insight that research and background knowledge can make to contributing to positive outcomes for children. Heather's case study provides a real-life scenario of a young boy and his family who find themselves during a challenging time. It provides an insight into how a multi-agency approach works to ensure the best outcomes for the child and the family, and Heather's role in coordinating the various professionals.

Heather Woodcock – Inclusion Manager

I have worked in a mainstream primary school and as a Children's Centre teacher, where I provided training for disengaged parents and increased my knowledge of multi-agency collaboration. Presently, I work for the Specialist Teaching service in Kent with an SEMH specialism. I engage with a range of professionals to achieve better outcomes for children with SEND needs. I see how positive parental engagement has a direct and beneficial effect on pupil behaviour and general outcomes.

Case Study:

Year 2 boy: Behaviour had escalated in school. My first job was to find out about his nursery experience. This, I learnt, was a struggle for him and staff, who had worked hard to manage his violent outbursts. They reported he targeted other children. He was also in Nursery every day for the most hours available and wasn't consistently dropped off and picked up by the same adults.

Parents: His challenging behaviour left parents blaming school; this relationship was strained. I set a home visit asking, if possible, for both parents to be present. At this point judgment of any sort needs to be suspended. My morals or value system are not a priority. I need to listen more than talk and ask questions honestly, putting the pupil at the centre of what I do. Parents both worked long hours and their son had less than an hour at the start and end of the day with them. At the weekend, he was not taken out as his behaviour was too challenging and parents admitted they couldn't manage him as they didn't feel confident with parenting strategies.

Specialist teacher: Multi-agency meeting held. Childcare was an issue and also parenting in the home. I worked with the Early Help worker to pass on successful strategies from school and as I had built a strong relationship with the mother I was able to discuss child development and how they could 'find' time for play and connection with their son rather than see their 'job' as a parent as giving him breakfast or putting him to bed. He was crying out for love and attention.

Early Help engaged to support in the home.

Educational Psychologist was commissioned to complete an assessment and I supported school to really 'see' the pupil, not just his challenges. As a teacher my core role is to improve educational outcomes by removing barriers and help with implementation of specific strategies.

A social prescriber from the local Doctors met with Mum. Supported her mental health by directing her to a group for support

Heather's Top Ten Tips:

1 Have an open mind when meeting parents and use a basic Maslow's Hierarchy of needs approach. Find out some background to the parents' current situation.

Strengthening links between schools and settings 51

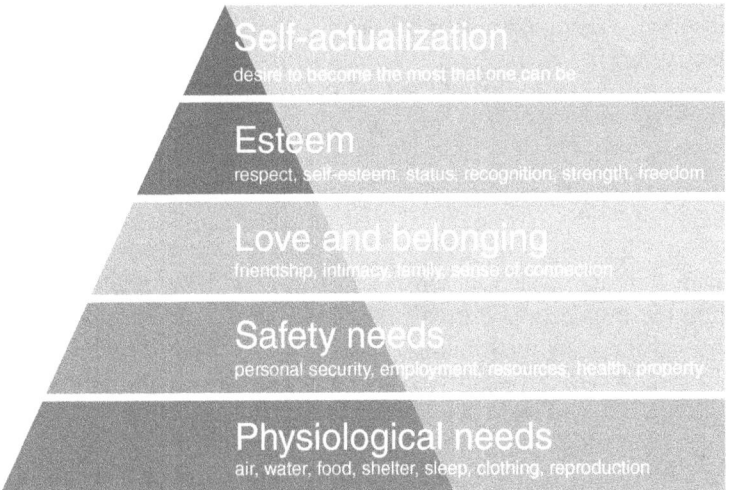

Figure 3.1 Pyramid of Maslow's Hierarchy of needs. This image supports Heather Woodcock's (Inclusion Manager) first tip, within her 'Top Ten Tips' section, for successful collaborations from her experience.

2 Think of parental links as being important in developing life skills for pupils, not just academic achievement.
3 Set boundaries to the times and ways of communicating. You need to protect your time.
4 Prepare scripts for difficult conversations (lateness, absenteeism, behaviour management techniques used in school and home) practise them with trusted staff.
5 Familiarise yourself with key school staff. The SENDCo, pastoral leads and FLO's have significant relationships with parents and multi-agency partners. Ask to observe key meetings.
6 See parents as experts on their own children and recognise that they often have high aspirations but possibly low skills in achieving them.
7 Recognise barriers, e.g. Is homework appropriate and, if so, are parents supported within school?
8 Listen more than speak. Listen for the relevant things that aren't being specifically talked about.
9 Your title is intimidating and a trigger for some parents. Be aware of their school experiences.
10 Be kind. Parents who are the most defensive or offensive and verbally aggressive often have the greatest worries and insecurities. As practitioners we need to be able to listen to them with kindness. It is reasonable to say, 'I can see how this is affecting you'. Remember it's not always you who is the reason for the anger, simply it can be what you are representing.

English as an additional language (EAL)

Collaborating successfully when all parties speak the same language can prove to be challenging enough. However, linguistic and cultural differences can, at times, place an additional perspective to navigate with regards to ensuring the reduction of barriers and full inclusion potential is met. It is important not to look at EAL as an additional area of collaboration; it must be included under the same umbrella as the rest of the whole-school inclusion policy.

The Conventions on the Rights of the Child states that children have clear rights to an education which develops their potential and enables them to achieve. Every child has rights, 'without discrimination of any kind, irrespective of the child's or his or her parent's or legal guardian's race, colour, sex, language, religion, political or other opinion, national, ethic or social origin, property, disability, birth or other status' (The UN Convention on the Rights of the Child, Article 2, 1990).

With so many potential collaborations, including EAL, there is a need to establish how we can develop these to be more successful, meaningful and robust – with every family, from every background. By interlinking the focus of working with EAL families into an existing 'Collaborative Policy', we ensure the continuous focus and duty of care as professionals, embedding the importance and structure throughout every part of a school's ethos and belonging within the school community.

Within the publication, 'Language development and school achievement' (Evan et al., 2016), the opportunities and challenges for students with EAL in education are discussed, sharing the identified importance of the relationship between school and families, "overall, school-home communication needs to focus much more clearly on the empowerment of parents, of which knowledge of the school system is a central factor. Empowerment also means that the school and staff reflect on 'outreach mentality" (Hamilton, 2013).

Wendy Cobb, Senior Lecturer at Canterbury Christ Church University, shares her knowledge and experience of EAL and the importance of identity, cultures and family traditions.

Wendy Cobb, Senior Lecturer – Canterbury Christ Church University

EAL – Being open to cultural identities and the importance of names

As a master's in education student, I was lucky to participate in an Erasmus initiative held in Murcia, Spain, along with groups of teachers and school leaders from England, Poland, Norway, Spain and Ireland. We were all working on our own research projects and, as a primary language specialist, my focus was on enabling democratic participation through the leadership of plurilingual and cultural awareness policies. My research mainly entailed gathering and analysing case studies arising through language-focused exchanges during the trip and led to the development of a policy audit tool. One unexpected encounter had a profound impact on my awareness of hidden cultural identities and on the approach to planning for primary languages and intercultural understanding teaching that I was developing with a group of Croydon schools. One English peer with a Brummie accent, who described herself as a 'non-linguist', revealed during a chance conversation the story of her own fascinating cultural heritage, explaining how her grandparents had emigrated to England from Italy to escape fascism and corruption. Her mum (born, as she described, in 'an Italian ghetto in Birmingham') never used her real name 'Anna', and instead adopted the Anglicised version 'Anne'. Although my peer's grandmother spoke Italian when her older siblings were growing up, her father didn't like it (my colleague thought this might be because of the link with fascism) so she herself knew only a few words in the language. She did not consider herself as bilingual, although she mused that she had named her cat Giovanni and later chose the pseudonym Salvatore to refer to her son in the transcript of our conversation. What I discovered through our one-way conversation (I listened, she talked) was an awareness of cultural identity and a rich linguistic heritage that emerged as she uncovered memories, such as Sunday lunch (a roast with a traditional tomato tart and whole artichokes) and the job she had of rolling gnocchi; something she didn't think anything of at the time, but now realised must have been a very unusual sight in most English homes back then. She also took strength from coming from what she termed as 'a line of women with a sense of injustice', recalling fascinating tales of her grandmother's and great grandmother's incarceration for treason during the First World War, and the general struggles and determination of her Italian forebears. Listening to my colleague uncovering her own story as she spoke, and recognising with pride the cultural traditions and family attributes that contributed to making the unique 'her', was a little like watching someone peeling the layers of an onion.

I have come to realise how important names are in shaping our identities and am conscious of how often people (including parents and children) too quickly accept new labels, either to make it easier for others to say their name or from a personal choice to hide their cultural identity.

By culture I refer not just to the experiences of non-native speakers, but also to the traditions, values and beliefs of other families who may feel like aliens in a school context. Getting to know each other is an important part of establishing a group identity within a welcoming class ethos and should include encouraging children to share their cultural experiences, since awareness of their cultural uniqueness is an important part of children's developing sense of self-identity. One of the strategies teachers can use is a focus on names, ideas for which Virginia Bower and I explore in our book *Language Learning and Intercultural Understanding in the Primary School*.

(Cobb and Bower, 2021 pp. 52–57)

Wendy's Top Ten Tips:

1. When you meet with your new classes, or talk to parents for the first time, take time to find out how to speak each child's/parent's name.
2. Ask children/parents what they prefer to be called.
3. Encourage children to tune into and practise unfamiliar sounds to help them have confidence to pronounce names correctly.
4. Find out as much as possible about children's existing linguistic knowledge and understanding and the different languages they speak.
5. Explore socially acceptable ways to address people formally and informally in different cultural and social contexts.
6. Be aware of the link between language and identity and children's sense of their place in the world.
7. Check your curriculum plans for cultural bias that privileges English as the most valued language.

8 Celebrate and overtly encourage continued home language use.
9 Have a focus on one language each month and invite children and their families to share their language and cultural traditions.
10 Reflect on how our identities are shaped by our families, the contexts in which we live and work and the similarities and differences between your own family traditions and those of your colleagues. Reflecting on own identities and the multitude of factors that shape them helps us to empathise with the diverse experiences of the children and families we meet.

Leadership and collaboration structures

As with listening to your school staff, it is important to think of the relationships with families and the school community as a connection and extension of your own team.

School leaders have a duty to create a culture inclusive to parents, families and the wider community, embedding this within the very essence of the school and with a narrative transparent to all, 'the importance of parent engagement in children's learning is widely acknowledged' (Goodall, 2017).

However, during my own research within my role as Parent Council Chairperson, it became apparent that not all leaders were confident with the idea of a parent council and the equal involvement that parents can have on the direction of the school. A narrative of 'They wouldn't understand', 'I wouldn't want to open that can of worms', 'How would that even work?' and 'We wouldn't have the capacity to manage that, we are already short staffed' emerged more often than I had initially expected.

To embrace and lead change, is to show courage and determination in areas others fear. Breaking the stereotypical mould of working with families, goes beyond symbolic activities such as coffee mornings (Auerbach, 2010); it is pushing the boundaries and encompassing a new way of working. This includes ways in which other professionals and educational settings collaborate – forming a significant role towards improving the communication culture.

Taking time to reflect, whether this be formally in a school improvement plan meeting or during an impromptu conversation in the staffroom, allows for breaks in the repetitive and windows of opportunity for the future. Reflecting on times of celebration and times of hardship help to shape future decision-making and offer a powerful resource to other leaders.

A report by the National College for Teaching and Leadership (2014) stated that outstanding primary leaders have, 'a strong sense of social justice, seeking to remove the barriers to achievement such as disadvantage and low parental aspiration by compensating for what the children lack and by working closely with families and community'.

Nicki Man reflects on her experience of leading a school during the COVID-19 pandemic and how the school adjusted to the needs of her families as the pandemic continued to impact her local community.

Nicki Man – Headteacher, Lydd Primary School, Kent

My school (like most others) faced new and unique challenges during the COVID-19 pandemic. As a school in an area of deprivation, the model of support being suggested by the government (with its images of families engaging quietly on a plethora of devices, in individual bedrooms, accessing home schooling, ably assisted by parents who completely understood the curriculum being offered) did not resonate with what we were experiencing in our community.

To add context, we have an Index of Multiple Deprivation of 63 out of 462, with 1 being the most deprived. However, we felt 'ahead of the game' when the pandemic threat loomed and the first lockdown approached, as we had already prepared quality packs of work to support our pupils. By pre-lockdown, half of our families were already isolating. We utilised an army of volunteers to ensure every home received their pack, in addition to providing work online.

This was where a journey began for all of us...

We discovered that many of our families had no devices to access the internet on at all. Multiple children were working from one mobile phone to try and access their individual online work. In other homes, there was simply no internet at all. With good intentions, we purchased dongles to remedy this, and provided devices to work on. However, this did not automatically mean that families suddenly understood how to use new technology, let alone being able to support their children!

By now, we were operating a small hub provision from our local secondary school for a handful of keyworker children. All other pupils were at home. We quickly realised that the concept of school had shifted from being a place primarily for education, to a centre of support and communication – a much-needed resource for our families, who, in some cases, had never felt so isolated.

We established a system where the school office was open during school hours to take calls and message requests. Additionally, we created a daily 'live hour', when parents could connect with their child's class teacher to be supported directly. Class blogs were set up to encourage older pupils to socialise with each other and write at the same time.

Three times a week, members of the team (including myself) walked around the locality responding to messages and requests for support. We delivered stationery (who knew stationery poverty was a thing until now?), provided a quick reassuring word from the end of the path to our pupils, dropped off bags of quarantined books and equipment, but, above all, spent time reminding them that we were still 'there' for them.

We listened and responded to what was needed in the moment. It was important to remember that what works for one may not for all. We surveyed our families and learned to our surprise that live lessons were not wanted – it was too constricting with lots of children in the home needing support! Parental preference was recorded content that could be rewatched and played at a time of their choosing.

Nicki's Top Tips:

- Be prepared to change and evolve – especially if an external situation is changing rapidly. What fits one week, might not work a month later! Go with it ... paperwork packs were not the answer for some of our children with SEN needs – they responded well to recorded content that they could replay in order to develop confidence with.

- Communication is key – lots of it in every way possible! Social media, parent mail, door to door, email… Find out what the barriers are to those not responding to you – is it a communication issue? Are they receiving your information? Communicating well and in a timely fashion supports great relationships with families.
- When we developed our home learning curriculum, we had to remember it is not a 'one size fits all' situation. Allow for flexibility in new projects – decide on the important 'non-negotiables' and key values to make it work, then work out where you have wriggle room.
- Get the right people, doing the right things – a more experienced or Senior Leadership Team member does not always equal 'best at'. New technology took us all by surprise – some of my least experienced staff members were quickly leading the way, flourishing as they took on new technology and supported other more experienced colleagues.
- Always take time to stop, evaluate and listen – what we might think is a good idea might not match what your community needs right now. We were worrying about how we could deliver more live teaching, when this wasn't what our community wanted or needed. Parent voice and surveys are key here!
- Keep an eye on the work–life balance for staff in new projects – it's easy to get carried away and unwittingly create a monster that adds work. Consider what can be removed as new initiatives are added. We also dropped in resources from other places such as Oak Academy if they fitted. Why re-invent the wheel?
- Stay calm – nothing frazzles parents like new technology, new ideas or work they don't understand. You can unwittingly become a target for this frustration – just keep in mind it's not personal; they simply want to do their best and not let anyone down. Find out the root of the anxiety and work together to resolve it, (I had a teacher demonstrating how to start up a new laptop outside the living room window – we got there in the end!).
- Look after yourselves – if the leaders and school staff are burnt out, they will have nothing left to offer anyone else. Check in with each other and make sure everyone is alright.
- Finally, stay true to the ethos and values of your school – we are a community-focussed, inclusive school and this approach ran deeply through our work with families. It was important to keep our identity alive, even in challenging times!

Nursery

Communication and collaboration often start before the first school bell rings. The latest data, reported by National Statistics (DfE, 2022), identified that in 2022, the number of 3- and 4-year-olds registered for the 30-hour entitlement and those in receipt of the Early Years Pupil Premium (EYPP) were the highest on record. With record numbers of children attending nursery, for many parents this would be the first experience of working with an educational setting. What happens at this stage helps to set expectations and the subconscious framework for all future educational collaborations.

> I had to return to work once my child was old enough to attend our local nursery at the age of 2. It was a really difficult decision to make and I felt really guilty about leaving him. We had a few options to choose from in the local area, so my husband and I visited each one.
>
> Immediately after leaving we would talk about the 'feel' of the nursery and the staff. We asked each other if we felt happy to leave our child with the adults in charge and whether we thought our son would like it there. My anxiety was high at the thought of leaving him. I didn't feel that he would cope well with separation and I also felt that he wasn't able to communicate as well as his peers.
>
> I made sure to share my concerns with staff and monitored their response. The nursery that we chose in the end had a speech and language playgroup service and the staff were skilled in communication difficulties. In addition to this, they ensured a very calm environment, centred around nurture.
>
> We liked the offer available at the nursery and also the specialist links established with other professionals. The Manager was able to talk about past experiences and I felt confident in their ability to work with us as parents and meet any needs that our son may display in the future. To us, it showed their ability to work well with others to achieve the best outcomes for the children. We couldn't ask for more and haven't looked back.
>
> *Parent Reflection*

Bethany, Early Years Practitioner and Nursery SENCo, reflects on her experience of working with parents and how best to support them during times of transition, support and engagement.

> **Bethany Dempsey – Nursery SENCo**
>
> Successful collaborations for working with families:
>
> I have worked in Early Years for 9 years with a range of different children and families. I have been an Early Years SENCo for 4 of those years. I have been very lucky to gain the trust of the families I have worked with and to help them to bring out the best in their child/children. From a SEN point of view, I have been able to take the time to speak termly with parents to discuss any concerns they may have and to offer support where needed. I feel that it is extremely important to speak to the parents in a way that they will understand and to explain every part of the EYFS to them in order for them to carry out similar support for their child/children at home. I have worked closely with a range of professionals, e.g. Specialist Teachers, Early Help Workers, Speech and Language therapists etc. To ensure that the needs of the children in my care have been met. For example, I have recently supported a child with ASD and PDA with a transition to school; this involved the specialist teaching and learning service and the child's family. As his Key Worker, it was part of my responsibilities to ensure a smooth transition to primary school through regular meetings with his new teacher and 1:1 support staff to ensure that they understood his needs and where they would need to adapt their school day to ensure that his needs were consistently met. It was very important that the child's parents were included as they felt very anxious

about their child moving to a new school. I accompanied the parents to stay and play events at the school to offer support and a friendly face that they could turn to.

I have been very lucky that I have been able to engage with and support these families. I am able to say that I have always had success when working with families and have never experienced any resistance for support.

Transitions:

When prospective parents come to look at our setting, we will send them home with an application pack. In this pack contains an application form and an 'all about me' form for the parents to fill in about their child. It will contain questions, such as nap times, bottle times, favourite activities, the child's level of speech, how they respond to being separated from their parent, religious preferences, behaviour and any other background information that would be useful for practitioners to know. We then invite the child to have a stay and play session at the nursery with their parent; this give practitioners the chance to talk over the 'All about me' form and to meet the child and parent. The child is then invited in for a short stay and play session without their parent. This is so that they can form a bond with their key person and to familiarise themselves with the setting. Families can access as many stay and play sessions as they would like to ensure that their child is settled into the setting.

Bethany's Top Ten Tips are aimed at parents and provide practitioners with the opportunity to reflect on their own practice when working with parents. Many of these tips are also relevant for children transitioning from nursery to reception, with approaches aimed towards improving children's wellbeing and educational outcomes 'close and respectful relationships with parents and the wider family have been seen as integral to young children's development' (DfE, 2010).

Bethany's Top Ten Tips:

1 Show your child pictures of the setting.
2 Talk positively about coming to nursery.
3 Make sure that your child is sent to nursery with any comforters, i.e. teddies or a dummy, as this can help settle the child if they become upset.
4 Show pictures of the nursery staff to your child so that they can become familiar with who will be looking after them.
5 Use social stories about coming to nursery – there are lots available online that are suitable.
6 Ensure that your child has a spare change of clothes, a coat and wellies, as well as nappies if they not potty-trained.
7 Always drop your child off with a smile – if they can see that you're anxious then they will be anxious too.
8 Always talk to the staff about any changes to your child's routine or development. They will ALWAYS help you.
9 If your child is anxious, explain to them step by step what will happen during the day. Nursery staff will help you with this if you do not know where to start.
10 Give your child lots of reassurance and praise for having a good day at nursery. This will help for the following session.

Primary

Most children in the UK start full-time education at the start of the school year in which they will reach school age (5 years old). The transition from pre-school to primary is a pivotal time for children and their families. New routines and relationships can all contribute to excitement and anxiety.

As we know, first impressions count, and the initial meeting between family and school is an incredibly important one. This first meeting gives the first impression to decide whether or not a family wants to send their child to your setting. This time provides the perfect opportunity for schools to outline their protocols with regards to working in partnership with families and what both parties (school and home) can expect as a result.

The transparency of the support for all – families, children and staff – helps to smooth transition and assist with a positive long-term relationship. This new period is not to be taken lightly, as it can be both vital and fragile, particularly within the infancy stages. Ensuring the correct foundations are in place will help to positively impact future relationships. As children progress through the school, from Early Years to Year 6, the relationships with their families will prove vital to a school's success – Have families been happy to stay with the school? Would they send additional siblings to your school? Would they recommend the school to other families?

By developing strong relationships between settings, positive relationships are more likely to succeed, 'The effectiveness and impact of multi-agency working is dependent on the quality and strength of the collaborative partnerships existing between services and the early years setting' (Cheminais, 2013). With this in mind, it begs the question – Should schools and nurseries adopt similar approaches, e.g. introducing a Parent Council? If every school and nursery had a consistent approach to parental engagement through parent councils, a huge element of support would be in place by the parents who would be able to provide peer-to-peer support, assistance with transition and the prerequisite of information sharing, decision making and support.

Niomi Clyde Roberts shares her ideology behind worthwhile investments with families and her own person experience of working with families within a primary setting.

Niomi Clyde Roberts – Assistant Headteacher, St George's Church of England Primary School

I think the most important part of the beginning of each academic year is establishing positive relationships with the parents of the children you teach. It is always worth putting in that extra time to make phone calls and to send a message over the school communication platforms, to ensure that the parents knows you are trustworthy and stick to your word. I know you're probably thinking 'They should already trust the teacher'; however, you are not aware of past experiences with previous teachers. Consistency is key and so is keeping that communication ongoing. When difficult conversations arise, there will be a mutual understanding, which means that inherently it will make these conversations easier to work through and keep that positive relationship afloat.

If parents have a question which they need answered I always try to ensure that I come back to them, as quickly as is realistically possible. If for any reason I can't, I will acknowledge their phone call or message and say that I will be in touch shortly. I find it's the tiny communicative details which can make all the difference. I am also a firm believer in sticking to your word; if you say you will follow something up, you should.

The children also benefit hugely from positive teacher and parent interaction because they can see that regular and constant communication; therefore, less misunderstandings and respectful relationships continue throughout the academic year and beyond. It is paramount that all educators make this a priority and remain open with communication. Parents will (at times) become emotional but always remember that often this because they are worried about something close to their heart.

Maintaining good relationships is as important as getting the learning right. It sets the climate for the year and it's well worth investing in.

Claire Frost shares her experience of successful transitions, her tried-and-tested approach to working in partnerships with parents and meeting the challenge of falling numbers in Early Years.

Claire Frost – Headteacher in Kent.

In 2015 I was seconded to lead a rural primary school which needed significant support to get back on track. The school was struggling in a range of areas but especially in Early Years, where pupil numbers had dropped to less than 50% of the much-needed intake. I took the substantive headship in 2016 and the school is now thriving and consistently over-subscribed for numbers in Reception. Communication with stakeholders has been key to our success and we have made a considered investment in our approach to transition from pre-school settings to school. We set early questions to reflect on for school development – How to effectively involve and share information with parents at transition? Were contributions from parents valued? How could we monitor and evaluate our transition offer to keep improving?

Our transition approach is responsive to cohort needs or contexts. This was especially necessary during the global pandemic where children had missed much of their nursery time and parental anxiety was high but can be for other reasons also, such as an incoming class with especially high levels of SEN. Considering all aspects of each incoming year group and being responsive to this has led settled transitions and then better outcomes.

Clear communication builds confidence in parents and children. Working in partnership is not an empty phrase, but something we put a high value on, and we recognised, without judgement, that families may be experiencing challenges which require support. Establishing this partnership begins when I meet prospective parents. I always visit parents myself to demonstrate my commitment to the importance of Early Years and to share my vision and passion for the education and wellbeing of their children. I ensure parents know what to expect from our Reception year and beyond; for example, we are an Outdoor Play and Learning (OPAL) school, meaning children may go home a little muddier from our outdoor play approach!

We proactively foster relationships with the nursery settings which has led to a reciprocal understanding of one another's ethos and values. Nurseries have invested in the children and naturally want them to progress to a school in which they will flourish. This building of strong relationships led to pre-school settings directly suggesting our school to parents who felt reassured by a recommendation from professionals they already trust.

New pupils' nursery experiences are highly varied, and we invest time to understand the approaches to learning in all settings. This, in turn, helps us appreciate parental choice and thereby what their expectations and aspirations for their child in school might be.

It also helped us understand formative experiences children have had when starting in our setting. The Reception teacher visits all children in their nursery to meet with the key worker and observe the child in a setting where they are settled and confident. This gives a better picture of the unique child and allows the teacher to plan for provision based on needs, starting points and interests.

Stay and Play sessions allow children to feel prepared for Reception class and, from April, children attending the local village nursery come for weekly story-time, so allowing them to become familiar with our school and for us to model our love of books. As soon as new pupils are confirmed, we are proactive in working with existing professionals involved with families and in engaging those we consider will be of benefit for transition. I participate in meetings for pupils with SEN so I am informed about needs and we can start planning as early as possible. This cements relationships with parents who may be feeling more vulnerable and demonstrates that I see their child as an individual.

As always in education, context is everything and I am fortunate to be surrounded by talented and committed teachers and support staff. Our strategies work for us and are either developed from evidence-based research or have been refined to have the best impact for the children we serve in our community. Our main aim is that communication with our families leads to a trusting and respectful partnership.

Claire's Top Ten Tips:

1 Make it clear from the beginning that it is a privilege to be entrusted with a child's education and how honoured you are that a parent has chosen your school. Communicate that you celebrate parents as a child's primary and most important educator. Ensure written communication is pitched to be accessible and welcoming.
2 Be transparent with parents about your school's vision, expectations and approach so they know exactly what choice they are making for their child and what the Reception year will look like.
3 Make strong connections with local nurseries and ask their advice on what they consider would be beneficial for transition practice. Listening to their voice led to one idea of inviting nursery staff to the first Christmas Play in school so they could see and celebrate the children.
4 Work with nurseries to develop a shared understanding of what school readiness looks like and how to support them in preparing for this.
5 We share personalised booklets (or videos) about the classroom, EYFS team and wider school for every child so they can look at it with parents over the summer. All new children are given a picture book and a Chatter Box. The book is the

first text shared in September, so children have that familiarity. Children fill the Chatter Box with special items they'd like to share with adults in school in Term 1. These offer a great way to encourage conversation and provide comfort for those children finding it harder to settle.

6 We moved from using the term 'Home Visits' to 'Getting to Know You' visits to the family home. A subtle change but it made a difference to parental perception and uptake. We offer these over the first two days in September as much can change over the six-week summer break.
7 Make sure your office team are invested in the transition process and understand its importance. They have considerable early contact with parents and will help form positive early relationships if they are approachable and informed. By the time of their first day in September, my families will be on first-name terms with my office manager and already comfortable to share concerns or ask questions.
8 Our SENCo invites all incoming parents to a SEN forum in the summer term along with the rest of our school parents. This provides information as well as helping new parents make links.
9 The Summer Term parent workshop, delivered by the Reception teacher, allows parents have an early understanding and active involvement in their child's learning journey and to better understand the role they play with school readiness.
10 Consider CPD for staff before the September start to set them and the children up for success. This might be specialised training based on individual pupil needs or in response to changes in local/national context for our youngest children. If appropriate, invite the parents to be part of or even deliver some of the training.

Secondary

The transition from primary to secondary is, without question, a huge step in a young person's life. It can be exciting and daunting, as farewells are made to the familiar and greetings are made to the new. If the emotions of the children are running high, the same could also be said for the parents and carers. Additionally, staff within school can also feel a mixture of anticipation, as a new cohort arrives and the responsibility of many new young faces filter through the doors.

It is in times of transitions that children need advocates to ensure the next step in their education runs smoothly. For some, it will be ensuring that their child knows how to navigate around the school and where they need to go for their first day. For others, there may be more complex needs to address which may involve additional members of the school team. Of course, parents can voice any concerns for their children but knowing who to talk to and how the support will present itself, can feel like a mountain to climb.

> "My child was nervous about whether he would have any of his friends in his class. He had to wait until he started in September to find out. I wanted a relaxing summer for him, but he spent the whole time worrying. If we had known the classes before the end of term, this would have really helped him – and me! I had underestimated his anxiety around this, and it put additional stress on us as a family".
>
> Parent, Kent

The enormity of achieving a smooth transition for all can feel like a mammoth task. The transition from primary to secondary can present itself as a delicate balance between settings, new school/old school, new protocols/current protocols, new friendships/old friendships.

Strength in collaboration and communication proves to be one of the key elements for success. The very meaning of the word collaboration itself derives from two Latin words – col (meaning 'together') and laborare (meaning 'to work').

Kerry Longman, Head of Year 7 at the Marsh Academy in Kent, shares her experience of successful transitions from primary to secondary. Kerry identifies how she works successfully with the children, their families and their primary schools, to ensure a seamless transition is achieved for all.

Kerry Longman – Head of Year 7

Marsh Academy, Kent

Having taught in both Primary and Secondary schools for several years, I am fully aware of the importance of getting the primary to secondary transition right. As Head of Year 7 for this year's cohort, this became my responsibility. I knew that a successful transition would lead to a successful start to the secondary school journey for these students. Although the main transition events for our students and parents began at the start of July, transition in general started much earlier.

In March, we contacted our feeder primary schools to arrange transition meetings. At this time, we requested key information about the students attending our school. This included Information such as Reading ages, 'Working at' levels and any other important information that we needed to be aware of.

In May, we met virtually with every feeder primary school. Each meeting typically involved myself as Head of Year 7, our SENCo, the Year 6 teacher(s) and the primary school SENCo. We discussed each child and how we could support their transition. For students who we agreed would benefit from additional transition, we offered 'Roving Reporter Tours' where they had an additional afternoon at school in a smaller group completing familiarisation tasks. Once these meetings had taken place, the Year 7 Team visited each primary school and met with the students where we talked to them about what they can expect from secondary school. This was a great opportunity for us to start getting to know the students and putting some faces to names.

In July, we held our Parent Information Evening. The Principal and I spoke to parents while students were organised into groups and given some activities to complete with their new peers; 'Getting to know you BINGO' and writing postcards to their tutors kept them busy and content but also enabled them to start getting to know one another. Refreshments followed and parents were able to talk to key members of the school community, such as our SENCo and Year team members. During this evening, we handed out important information to parents about policies, expectations and uniform. We also provided all students with a Summer Reading book. Staff members from our school recorded a chapter of the book and this was uploaded to the school website. This was then used as the theme for some of our Tutor time activities in Term 1.

During the same week as the parents' evening, students completed their two-day induction period where they had a taster of secondary school.

My experience of Year 6 taught me that it is not just students who are anxious about transition; often parents are equally as, if not more, anxious than the students themselves. Some parents will have had negative experiences of school and for this reason, I wanted to do as much as I could to start building in opportunities for our new parents to come in to school and meet with us, to see that we are approachable and genuinely here to help. As well as the parents' evening, we also arranged coffee mornings. One was held at our school and then one at our larger feeder primary school. Both were well attended and gave us a chance to connect with our new parents and welcome them to our community.

One very successful part of our transition was our Summer School. During the Summer break there are fewer staff and no other students on site which allows full use of the school and facilities. Our focus for summer school this year was team building and problem solving. Across four days, our activities were all designed with this in mind and included tasks such as: team-building challenges (marshmallow and spaghetti bridges, Sellotape and paper towers); orienteering around the school site; origami tasks; and science investigations, as well as some more academic lessons too. In addition to sessions run by our teaching staff, we also invited the Army who led an activity day focused on problem solving where students completed a range of activities. They had to carry heavy army equipment, across platforms – working together they directed blindfolded 'soldiers' across a minefield, collecting equipment as they went. It was wonderful to see students working so well with each other, building trust and beginning to make friendships.

In addition to the activities on site, we organised a trip to a local activity centre where students were able to participate in a range of activities, including archery and rock climbing – again, a focus on pushing them outside of their comfort zone and working collaboratively.

It was an incredibly successful week and 98% of the students who attended said they either agreed or strongly agreed that they were feeling more confident to start school because of Summer School and we were delighted to see that 100% said that they had enjoyed the week and would recommend it to future Year 7 students.

As a result of the success of our transition and Summer School, the start to the academic year has been very positive. Throughout the many transition events we offered, students learnt about our expectations of behaviour, how to conduct themselves as they move around the school, and how to work collaboratively and problem solve. More importantly, however, we got to know them and some of their parents. Making these connections early on will hopefully support us in continuing our journey with much success.

Kerry's Top Ten Tips for Transition:

1 Start transition as early as possible. Arranging meetings with local feeder primaries and trying to synchronize dozens of calendars is tricky. It is also worth checking the date of KS2 SATS assessments so that you can avoid making appointments around this time.

2. Involve key staff members; SENCo FLO, Safeguarding leads. The more people who can attend the initial meetings, the better. Ensure communication between this group of staff is consistent and everything is shared.
3. Remember that not all parents will have had positive experiences of school themselves and they may feel incredibly anxious as a result. Try to change this perception by showcasing how amazing the school is, sharing success stories and inviting them in.
4. Create opportunities for informal meetings. Coffee mornings are a great way to do this and if you can hold these at the local feeder primaries, ask a few members of their school staff to attend – this really helps to 'break the ice' and they can support with introductions.
5. At any parent event, take a notepad and pen. Parents will take this opportunity to tell you everything about their child – jot key information down and follow up if need be. If you are caught without, ask them politely to follow it up in an email which you can respond to later.
6. Consider running a Summer School. For us, this was one of the most successful parts of our transition. We ensured a range of activities, with a focus on having fun, getting to know the school site, building relationships and teamwork. All of which helped to ensure that our students were ready for their first day of school.
7. Take advantage of primary school newsletters. Most primary schools have their own class pages online – if you want to promote a Parents' Evening, Coffee Morning or Summer School – ask them to add it to their newsletters or pages. This way, your information will trickle through to parents from all different angles.
8. If you are given information regarding students with challenging behaviour, work out who they are straight away and try to catch them being good and praise them at every (genuine) opportunity. Some of these students may have found themselves stuck in a loop of negativity, and a positive comment might be all they need to hear. Remember, this is a chance for a fresh start for everyone.
9. Consider hosting a writing moderation for your feeder primary schools. We found this was a useful way for our English teachers to see the work students were completing at the end of Year 6. We also ask students to bring a piece of English writing with them when they come for their induction day. This is then passed on to their new English teacher.
10. Talk with primary schools about how they can support your transition. Is there anything you would like the new Year 7s to be able to do? Once SATS are out of the way, Year 6 teachers will most likely appreciate a few additional tasks to focus their 'Secondary School ready' classes. If you are given information regarding students with challenging behaviour, work out who they are straight away and try to catch them being good and praise them at every (genuine) opportunity. Some of these students may have found themselves stuck in a loop of negativity, and a positive comment might just be all they need to hear. Remember, this is a chance for a fresh start for everyone.

Special Educational Needs (SEN)

With increased parental involvement, the work between professionals, schools and families becomes even more effective. The narrative of 'must', within the SEND Code of Practice (2015b), emphasises just how important it is to work collaboratively between home and school.

> "Where a setting identifies a child as having SEN, they must work in partnership with parents to establish the support the child needs." SEND Code of Practice
>
> (2015b: 5.3)

Research conducted by the Education Endowment Foundation (2020) looked at how schools should effectively engage parents of children with SEND, identifying how, in many cases, perception can vary with huge impact: 'There was some difference in perception of service delivery between education professionals and parents; parents believed they received little help or information, while education professionals believed they supported parents across the school years' (Roberts and Simpson, 2016, p. 1091).

The Lamb Report (2009) specifically looked at school relationships with parents, setting a baseline for how schools should be working with families. The report stated the importance of inclusion for all, identifying that whichever stage of education a child is in, the importance of communication remains key for successful outcomes: "In the most successful schools, the effective engagement of parents has had a profound impact on children's progress". This notion supports the statement within the SEND Code of Practise (DfE, 2015b), which describes one key area of focus to be inclusive practice, and the importance of removing barriers to learning.

A significant milestone in a young person's life is the transition between settings, with moving from primary to secondary as one of the most significant transitions many would have made in their life so far. This transition can be even more monumental for children that have been in a mainstream during their primary years, and then move onto a SEN school for secondary.

Emma Read, SENCO and Teacher at the Marsh Academy, shares her experience of working within a mainstream secondary school with a specialist onsite SEN provision. Emma shares her experience of working with families and children to enable successful outcomes, smooth transitions and fully supported start to secondary school life.

Emma Read – SENCO and Teacher. Marsh Academy Secondary School, Kent

Currently, we start our transition process within the SEND department from September/October prior to the new intake coming to the Academy. We complete a range of tours for perspective EHCP students and parents. We discuss the provision available and the children's specific needs. At this point we haven't usually received copies of EHCP documents and consultations. Consultation requests usually start from November. This year all consultations have been sent as a bundle following the secondary transfer meetings at the Local Authority. Once consultations have been completed, we await a response from the Local Authority. The mainstream SEN transition process starts in Term 3 when discussions start with feeder primary SENDCOs.

Last year, I completed a short presentation at the Shepway SENCO Forum outlining the mainstream and SRP provision at the Academy. We discussed the range of interventions available, and shared information about the facilities that we have. Primary SENDCOs were provided with time for Q&A and our Contact details. Following this meeting we received many requests for meetings and additional transitional support.

I set up many virtual meetings accompanied sometimes by the SRP lead to discuss both students with EHCPs and other 'high-profile' students. Meanwhile the whole-school transition information gathering had commenced and additional students on primary school SEN registers identified. Once these meetings were complete, we set up further contact with some of our primary SENDCO links. One primary school organised an afternoon of virtual meetings with the primary schools EP, the students' parents and myself, where we discussed specific information required for transition and created an action plan and pen portrait to support transition.

In the case of another primary school we organised a weekly check-in via teams for a vulnerable student with their new keyworker. This enabled the member of our team to get to know the student ahead of the transition days and for their anxieties be alleviated. We organised a range of 'roving reporter' tours with small groups of students. These students toured the school with me and a member of SEN. The worksheet contained a range of questions about the school and the children during the tour could ask anyone for the answers. Upon completion, the children returned to their classes at primary school and shared their knowledge. Some created PowerPoints from the photographs taken on the tour and some presented their answers.

Maintaining good relationships with existing parents/families.

It is an integral part of the SENDCo role to keep parents informed. We work alongside a range of outside agencies and our Provisions team. I personally believe that good relationships are key. Our parents value phone calls, meetings (both virtual and face-to-face) and an email response. We always aim to respond within 24–48 hours to a parent so that any questions can be answered promptly. Our parents value honesty and like to have a clear plan that can be reviewed. Even when the plan has to be adapted, keeping parents informed is key and working together is paramount.

How support systems are developed and used within the Marsh Academy Community Hub (MACH) with regards to building/maintaining relationships with SEND children and their families.

An open-door policy is generally used. We welcome parents to the building to see how the SEN teamwork with our students. They see the facilities. We offer a time-out facility for the children, where they can exit lessons to gain support from a familiar member of the SEN department. We have a key worker morning check-in and afternoon check-out in place for students that require it as part of their provision. A familiar adult that they can talk to morning and afternoon. We provide a nurture provision for some students. This is delivered as both a morning check-in, where our nurture staff will talk to the individual students whilst eating breakfast, and a twice-weekly group intervention, which mirrors a family setting. The importance of positive relationships for all involved and how this impacts staff/families/children.

This is key. All working together enables a plan to be implemented, supported and adjusted when necessary so that the child is successful and reaches their potential.

> **Emma's Top Ten Tips:**
>
> 1 There is no I in team! This is my department motto and I repeat it frequently for all to hear.
> 2 Be a SEND co-ordinator and not a SEND do it all.
> 3 Trust your team.
> 4 Remember always to have a good work–life balance. Wellbeing is key – don't be scared to ask for someone to talk to. Supervision sessions can enable you to leave work with a clear head space.
> 5 Make sure that you use and share a good diary system with your team.
> 6 Meeting minutes and typing up your notes are invaluable when you need to look back at things several months later.
> 7 Remember that Quality First teaching (QFT) happens in the classroom. Teachers are responsible and should be accountable for meeting the needs of all learners.
> 8 Make friends with your Provisions Team. Your Provision Evaluation officers (PEOs) are invaluable for advice and support.
> 9 Remember to say thank you to your team, school admin, attendance, maintenance and catering teams as they will make your life so much easier. Kindness goes a long way!
> 10 Make sure that you employ someone who makes a great cup of tea/coffee!

Trainee teacher programmes

It would seem somewhat criminal not to go back to the very start of a teacher's career and look at the training and experiences designed to shape professionals that have the privilege of working with children and young people.

Placements, The National Curriculum, the history of education and differing ideologies, reflections and portfolios are just a few of the areas covered within current training programmes. Whilst relationships and the importance of building and maintaining professional integrity are covered as part of the course, it could be said that more could be identified and taught around the topic of parental engagement; the importance of building, maintaining and developing relationships successfully, managing challenging conversations and understanding the wider impact of successful partnership working.

> I was so excited to meet my first class – I was fresh out of uni and ready to go! I spent the summer preparing the classroom and my first few lessons. The only thing that really made me feel nervous, was the expectations of the parents and working with a TA who was the same age as my mum (many more years my senior and much more experienced than I was in the school). I had spent so long thinking about working with the little people, that I hadn't realised how anxious I would feel about working with the big people! – Teacher

> When I started my teacher training, my mind boggled at the broad range of terminology and acronyms. I remember a more experienced teacher laughing about the

> world of education being like 'another world with its own language'. He said, with time, I would understand them all – and I did. However, we, as educators, are creating an immediate wall of hostility and power over parents who do not understand this language. What adds to this confusion and an already complex area, is the interchangeable language used between organisations and settings. I have seen it contribute towards barriers in my school. – Primary Teacher

Wendy Cobb shares her advice and experience for trainee teachers completing their training, from appropriate communication to authentic partnerships.

Wendy Cobb – Canterbury Christ Church University

Menu of Learning Opportunities for Working with Parents/Carers on Placement

The first parents' evening of the year can be quite daunting for early career teachers. I don't recall any guidance about working with parents during my own PGCE studies and the only parents' evening tips I had from my mentor were, 'Make sure to let them ask their own questions first, otherwise you'll run out of time', and 'Remember, they're probably more scared of you than you are of them'. Luckily, I had both age and parenting experience on my side. I was in my mid-thirties with two young children when I qualified and parents in my first school assumed that I was an experienced teacher. I had plenty of tales of my own parenting failures to share and could express genuine empathy with some of their struggles. I wish I had known as a young mum the positive parenting strategies I later learned through my research collaborations with emotional health and parenting experts.

Roll on several years and I was leading a 'working with parents/carers' workshop on a School Centred Initial Teacher Training course when I discovered that many of the trainees attending had been given limited, if any opportunities to engage with families. They had been exposed to some theory, but most had not had the opportunity to experience theory in action. Some trainees implied that their school considered them 'too dangerous' to be let loose on parents and talked of being banned from the playground at the start/end of day. Schools might rightly argue that it is much easier to break than to build positive partnerships with families and communities, so this reluctance to let trainees meet parents is perhaps understandable. Some students did, however, have more positive experiences, particularly in schools where they were recognised as integral members of the teaching team, albeit in training. Some trainees were encouraged to write a letter home to introduce themselves to families and some had been encouraged to take the lead in parents' evening conversations. These discussions led us as a group to ponder the experiences that teachers might need before qualifying.

The trainees decided on some essentials:

- Be introduced to parents (for example, the trainee letter home idea, or a mention in the school newsletter/social media page)
- Share a child's effort/achievement (such as a note home/an invitation to the classroom to look at work)

- Contribute to a pupil progress report
- Engage with parents/carers in the classroom/playground at the end of the day
- Observe, contribute to or role play a meeting with parents

and some possible ideas that trainees might initiate such as:

- Create a welcome pack for the parents of a new EAL pupil
- Contribute to a news item hosted on the school website/newsletter.

We then thought about the skills, knowledge and understanding that teachers might need for authentic communications and began to mind map some prompt questions that might help such as,

- 'What are appropriate means of communication?'
- 'Are you using plain language which clearly communicates what you want to say?'
- 'Are meetings at a time when most parents can attend?'
- 'How will you build the trust of the parents?'
- 'Have parents been given enough information so that they can prepare for the meeting?'
- 'Can the child be involved in the meeting? If not, have you found out their point of view before the meeting?'

These activities and prompts were then further developed with contributions from parenting experts and special school leads into a Menu of Learning Opportunities (MoLO) for building authentic partnerships with parents and carers on placement, which we have continued to update with current research findings.

Wendy's Top Ten Tips

Trainee Teachers and Training Programmes

Building authentic partnerships with families is a complex challenge for schools, but there are some useful tips for early career teachers that I have gathered from working with both trainee teachers and parenting experts:

1 Walk around the boundaries of the school and get a feel for the community.
2 Hide sticky note messages about children's achievements in the home/school reading journal. This works particularly well for children who get embarrassed by public praise and is an opportunity to build a trusting relationship with both the child and the family.
3 Think of parents as the experts of their children – you are not expected to know more about them than they do.
4 Value the diversity of cultures and the uniqueness of every family.
5 Try not to pre-judge (you might want to remember me, both failing parent and parenting lecturer!).

6 Value the angry parent as someone who cares and be open to difficult feelings, including your own.
7 Show that you are actively listening. For instance, with an anxious parent you might say, 'You sound really worried about this'.
8 Empathise.
9 Practise the 'sorry, glad, sure' calming response which demonstrates that you recognise parents' and children's feelings and anxieties and helps to avoid adopting a defensive response. 'I'm sorry to hear that Josh is upset. I'm glad you have brought this to my attention. I'm sure that we can find a solution to make things better….'
10 Reframe what you can influence. You will often feel powerless to change the home circumstances of vulnerable children and parents, so think about what you can control, such as how you respond to a child at school who may be finding it difficult to concentrate or the anxious parent waiting at the office.

Home links and COVID-19

During usual circumstances, links with home are conveyed through the more 'traditional' methods – talking to parents daily at the classroom door, contact with parents at drop-off and pick-up, Headteacher on the gate, TA on the door, trip to the school office, messages in home/school books – patterns generally familiar to most families.

However, collaborative working with families took an incomparable turn once the pandemic hit in 2020. Suddenly, we were all on an equal playing field, with the field looking rather large, unfamiliar and intimidating – for parents, students, teachers and school leaders, the road ahead was uncertain. We all faced a new and challenging situation, all wanting to do the best for the students but none of us having any previous experience on how best to achieve this.

Teachers worried about meeting the needs of their children – educationally, emotionally and from a welfare perspective. The emphasis was now on the parents, who were facing an equally challenging and worrying time. Sue Atkins reflects on the innovative strategies schools created to be able to support children and the vital role that families had during a time of unprecedented uncertainty.

Parent Involvement Has Always Mattered.

But Will The COVID-19 Pandemic Finally Make This the New Normal?

Sue Atkins – The Parenting Expert

The global pandemic has changed life as we know it around the world in so many ways, from working from home in lockdowns to the new normal of juggling hybrid working and family life.

With families, schools and children having had to adapt to home schooling, or home learning, everything changed. School closures and remote learning propelled children's ability to learn independently to the forefront of every busy and stressed-out parent and teacher's wish list. Some schools adapted quicker and with more agility than others, but the overriding focus was on making sure families had everything they needed for their children to learn, and to offer families whatever support they needed during the crisis.

But why did it take a global health crisis to get to this point?

Until the coronavirus pandemic, the global education community spent comparatively little time thinking about the role of parent engagement in education.

But in March 2020 – the month when almost all of the world's countries shut their school doors – engaging parents moved quickly to the top of the agenda. Educators and education leaders around the world developed new and creative ways of substantially engaging parents in their children's learning.

These innovative strategies emerged out of necessity, but they are likely to prove highly beneficial to children long after we come through the pandemic. The evidence around family engagement in education shows that more trusting relationships between families and schools have been developed and are an essential foundation for building productive partnerships going forward.

It also shows that parents and caregivers can be an important ingredient in a child's achievement in school. When parents are involved and supportive of their children's learning at home by, for example, asking questions and showing an interest in their children's schoolwork, all children (but especially children who are from marginalised and low-income communities) – benefit. With involved and interested parents at home, children are more likely to attend, complete, enjoy and do well in school.

'There is no smaller classroom than a family's kitchen and there's no better way to personalise a child's learning than through their parents.' – Sue Atkins

It's about relationships – teachers and parents building a positive relationship, setting some goals, and making a game plan together – all with one simple goal: The child's best interest at the centre of the relationship.

It's about creating a 'new normal' and building bridges, not walls, between home and school, encouraging, partnering, and supporting parents and teachers to work together.

One of the key members of staff that work closely with families is the Family Liaison Officer. Their role involves managing attendance, preventative work, early intervention activities, supporting families in need, making referrals to outside agencies when required and working to close the gap in terms of underachievement.

Changing the narrative

It is important to reflect on current practice. It is easy to fall into the habit of repeating behaviours, especially when things appear to be working well. However, a fresh perspective and review of the current approach to collaborating with families can prove to be a very worthwhile exercise. Lucy Griffiths realised shortly after joining her school's Senior Leadership Team, that communication with parents could be improved, turning the negatives into positives.

Lucy Griffiths – Primary Teacher

With regard to relationships with parents, as a school, we've put a few things in place. Parents' evenings, as soon as we could, have been face-to-face. We have an open evening at the end of each academic year where we serve wine and soft drinks

> in the hall and the parents are greeted by the headteacher and then they wander off with the drinks in hand to go and visit the new classrooms and new teachers and previous teachers too. We invite parents in for workshops and welcome meetings where there will always be a bar where people can get a drink and then chat amongst each other and the staff, which again means that we have a good relationship that way. The one thing when I started on the Senior Leadership Team that I was very aware of was the fact that we only ever rang parents when there was something negative. Either the children were ill or they had done something wrong and I really wanted to change the way that we interact with them by phone, so I introduced the 'feel-good Friday' phone call. Every Friday, a teacher chooses at least one child (it can be as many as they want) to phone the parent to let them know that the child has had a great week and it has been probably one of the most positive things we have done with parents. It's opened up conversations; it's made parents really appreciative of what we do; and I think that the staff get a real buzz from this as well so it's like win-win.
>
> We are very inclusive of parents on the PTA, we have fetes and fayres, where they run stalls. We have lots of parent helpers too. We are a small primary of 210 and not to sound cheesy but it's like a big extended family. The teacher who had been there the shortest time has been there 8 years, the longest 30, and the rest of us somewhere in between.
>
> Parents are encouraged to listen to their children read and respond – it's expected and, on the whole, this happens. We respond in reading records to parents too. There's an open-door policy to all of us – if you need to speak to us, we will always be available, so things don't fester. This helps, I think, as you can nip things in the bud.

The 'Invisible links'

Whilst the more obvious links are between schools, agencies and specialist provisions, there are many other avenues and outlets to explore where engagement has generated positive outcomes with families.

Not only have these outlets provided opportunities for children to develop social and communication skills, it has also provided essential links for families and schools by providing unique opportunities for collaboration between the school and with peers.

Whilst the list of possibilities is extensive, this section will look at the outcomes possible from developing your own on-site Forest School Toddler group, PTFA and volunteering opportunities. These additional areas not only support your child's school but also capture wonderfully unique experiences for all, captivating the hearts of the whole school community and championing community projects.

Forest School Toddler group

Firstly – do not be fooled by the name! If you have your own woodland – wonderful. If you have a small patch of land – that'll do just as well. Outdoor learning, wellbeing opportunities and being in nature, are undisputed areas that can benefit us all. Additionally, it provides a space for creativity, imperfection, risk taking, exploration, adventure and opportunities for every age and ability.

The aim of the group for primary schools is to achieve success in the following areas:

- Aid the new intake for children starting in our reception class.
- Build relationships with new and existing families.
- Identify areas for improvement and development for the school.
- Provide a service to families within an area of deprivation, where transport and groups are limited.
- Identify needs of families and work collaboratively to provide support and assistance where required.

Forest School Toddler Group

Teacher and Forest School Toddler Group Leader

We wanted to engage with local families and provide an experience for pre-school children. The aim of the group was to encourage new and existing families, to help build relationships for our new September intake and finding ways that we could support our local families.

The group was really successful. The FLO would attend, along with myself and through informal chats and conversations, we were able to identify any needs and develop new relationships.

We received a high number of father attendees who said that they felt the group was 'less intimidating' than traditional toddler groups. One father said that it was the only other toddler group he had been to, other than football tots. They liked the freedom of being outdoors, the flexibility to move around in open space and the opportunity to be creative in nature (mud pies, mud slides and muddy puddles galore!).

I would recommend all schools to start a Forest School Toddler group with any available open space. I can be a project that can develop and grow over time. Our sessions ran for 1 hour, with free-play opportunities, craft activity, mud kitchen, story-time and drinks and snacks for all.

The staff as well as the parents, commented on how lovely it was to be outside and in nature – "It recharged my batteries!".

We advertised the need for materials and welcomed any free labour from parents that would be willing to make anything from a mud kitchen to a bird feeder. As part of the sessions, we would plant, grow and nurture the space. It became a place that everyone felt a sense of ownership towards.

Waterproofs and wellington boots are the only essential. Have fun and make it your own!

Forest Group Toddler Group

Ten Top Tips:

1 Use any outdoor space possible. You do not have to have a designated forest school area. Clear a space and utilise what you have.

2. Ask families for help and donations – A mud kitchen is simple to set up, it can be as fancy or as basic as you like (the kids prefer the basic versions where they get to change it and use their own imagination). An old washing-up bowl, table, discarded pots and pans and a few wooden spoons are enough to get started. Just add mud and water! PTFA fundraisers can help with basic equipment such as child size wheelbarrows and gardening tools.
3. Provide different places for children and parents to sit and explore. A private seat away from the rest of the group, might be just what one parent needs to feel able to confide in you.
4. Bring everyone together at the end – Story time around the 'campfire' was one of the most requested parts of the session.
5. Pinterest will be your best friend – Look for nature-themed crafts that won't cost much and are wonderfully inspiring.
6. Ask for a donation, rather than having a set price to attend. This ensures the group is accessible to all.
7. Have a blueprint idea for the sessions and change accordingly for special events/time of the year. We always had two craft activities, the mud kitchen and story time.
8. Offer refreshments. We had water and squash for the children, tea and coffee for the adults and a selection of fruit and biscuits. For some parents, this was the only time they got to have a hot drink with another parent and talk about their challenges and experiences.
9. Share information about the school gently. Encourage different members of staff to attend the group, even if it is just for 10 minutes to say hello and to experience the group. It helps build relationships between families and staff. Staff benefit from seeing the group and are able to talk to families about it.
10. Share the success and photos on social media. One father came after seeing other fathers in a photo. Link with other local settings and tell them about your group.

PTFA and volunteering

PTFA

Most schools have a Parent, Teacher and Friends Association (PTFA), which is a collective group of parents, staff and associated people, such as extended friends, family and community members, that work together to make the school a better place for the children through fundraising and events. PTFAs vary from school to school, but research conducted by Parentkind, identified their main roles to be; raising funds or resources, holding events and activities to develop the school community, enhance communication between parents and school and helping parents to have a voice at school (Parentkind, 2022).

Dr Emily Lau shares her experience as a parent on her time as a PTFA member, reflecting on areas of success and opportunities.

Dr Emily Lau

Being a part of my children's school community has always been a priority to me, both as a parent, but also as an active volunteer within my community – I grew up in a small town with a well-connected local school and I believe school experiences are enriched by strong relationships and contributions from local families and organisations. Ensuring my children and their peers benefit has always been important. My experiences of PTA, school fundraising and voluntary action have been mixed at the schools my children have attended. Fundraising is regularly requested both for the school and other causes, without much information. Sometimes it has clearly been done in partnership with the children, which I like. PTA involvement has tended to be chaotic and participated in by a small number of parents – as lives get busier, this seems to limit parents' and carers' regular commitment. Other opportunities to participate in learning events, decision-making and school activities are sporadic and one-off. As part of the parent and carer community I feel like parents have ideas about the way their children learn and the experiences they have, but this does not translate into action. I'd like to see more dialogue between school, parents and carers in order to understand better some of the decisions schools make. In one school, the PTA group met with the Head every Monday instead of only meeting to arrange Christmas or summer fairs. This led to a better and consistent role for parents and carers within the school and also brought about more transparency about how budgets were being spent, activities were being chosen and learning was being enhanced.

Breaking the mould and captivating communities

Whilst the majority of schools follow similar strategies to engage with their families and communities, embracing the unique and unlocking the potential can bring exciting opportunities for all. Dave McPartlin shares a personal experience from Flakefleet Primary School, along with his 'Top Ten Tips', encouraging others to take a leap of faith and try something new.

Dave McPartlin – Head Teacher, Flakefleet Primary School

Going for Christmas No.1 probably isn't what most people think of when they think about raising the aspirations of a school community, but our ridiculous adventure did just that, as well as landing us a Top 40 and so much more. When we changed our school Facebook page name to 'Flakefleet Primary for Christmas No. 1', back in December 2018, I'm sure most people thought we had lost the plot and were getting just a little carried away. We absolutely were – with no apologies for doing so. We wanted to show our community that it was OK to think big, dare to dream and not worry about what other people think when you pursue a goal that nobody else thinks you can achieve. Too often, we filter our ambitions by what we think we can afford, what people will say and how we look – there was no risk of us falling into this trap over the festive season. We put a shout out to see what expertise we had in our community and wider area using our social media channels and, surprisingly quickly, we found ourselves a recording studio courtesy of our local high school and some local musicians who could help us put our own song together. The children and staff put the lyrics together, every child in the school was on the track and we even managed to take residents of our local care home out on a day trip to Blackpool to record the pop video – within a few weeks, 'Light Up' was born and our epic mission was well underway. The sense of belonging and community that was being created was palpable and we knew something exciting was happening. There are lots of kind people out there in the world, who often just need an opportunity to get involved and help make a positive difference to the lives of our children.

We were quickly inundated with generous offers of printing, transport, advertising and so much more. Parents turned up at the weekend to hand out leaflets in the community, as well as taking them much further afield to cities across the north. We even bagged ourselves a Battle Bus and our children enjoyed adventures across the UK, gate-crashing Chris Evans and Radio 2 as well as *Good Morning Britain* and *The One Show*. Parental engagement was through the roof and social media was awash with positive messages of support; even Stephen Fry got involved at one point. Christmas 2018 was as ridiculous as it sounds and, ultimately, we were nowhere near the top spot, despite being third favourite with the bookies and third in the downloads for the Christmas week charts. We learned the true value of reliance and perseverance.

For a short time, we really thought we could do it and, I have to admit, with a little more luck, I think we could have done but, in many ways, the chart position was irrelevant. We had so much fun, a community came together like a lower league team's cup run and we were united in our excitement – we belonged to something special. Going for the festive top spot isn't for everyone, but it worked for us. Our audacious attempt played to our strengths and showed what can happen when you turn your aspirations to the max, dare to dream and just got for it – what might it look like in your world?

Dave's Top Ten Tips:

1 Think big and turn it up – Whatever you are thinking of doing, what would it look like if you gave yourself permission to get totally carried away? Most people probably thought we couldn't have a huge festival and fireworks display at school but over 1,000 children and their families turned to see that we definitely could!
2 Novelty value – Bingo nights and coffee mornings are great and there is an absolute place for them, but what about trying something different? Making it snow at our Carol Service didn't cost very much but created priceless memories.
3 The experience – From start to finish of whatever you come up with, think about what it will be like for the family. Keeping to times, making things look the part and considering the actual experience is essential – we've used music, balloons and street entertainers to liven up many an event.

4 Cheap – The more expensive something is, the higher the expectations. Always under-promise and over-deliver, sending people away thinking that an event was such good value.
5 Not everything has to cost – Use your position as the centre of the community to bring people together. Family picnics, trips to the beach or just a game of rounders can all be put together quickly and easily with minimum effort.
6 Use social media – Advertise using your social media channels and don't be afraid to ask people for support – there are lots of kind people out there who love an opportunity to help their community.
7 Parent power – Get your families involved in the organisation of events; you won't always be aware of how much they appreciate the chance to socialise or build their skills base – we've had many parents go on to get jobs on the back of their experiences getting involved with the school.
8 Listen to the parents – Ask them what they would like to do, some of our best (and often most simple) ideas have come from parents. Ask them what they think of the offering for parents, do more of what they like and less of what they don't!
9 Keep it varied – Not everyone likes loud music or to have a drink. Think about how you are appealing to your range of parents as it is easy to slip into the habit of only appealing to one demographic.
10 Have fun! – It sounds daft, but enjoy the moment, be yourself and let your hair down. Parental engagement activities are a great way of letting families see the real you and it's great for building relationships as well as being good for your own wellbeing.

References

Auerbach, S. (2010). Beyond coffee with the principle: Toward leadership for authentic school-family partnerships. *Journal of School Leadership*, 20(6). https://doi.org/10.1177/105268461002000603

Cheminais, R. (2013). Effective multi-agency partnerships. Accessed 14th June 2022. https://doi.org/10.12968/eyed.2009.11.3.42743

Children Act. (2004). Accessed 12th January 2023. https://www.legislation.gov.uk/ukpga/2004/31/contents

Cobb, W. and Bower, V. (2021) *Language Learning and Intercultural Understanding in the Primary School: A Practical and Integrated Approach*. Oxon: Routledge.

Evan, M., Schneider, C., Arnot, M., Fisher, L., Forbes, K. and Liu, Y. (2016). Language development and school achievement. Accessed 7th February 2023. https://www.educ.cam.ac.uk/research/programmes/ealead/Executive_Summary.pdf

DfE. (2022). Education provision: Children under 5 years of age. Accessed 7th February 2023. https://explore-education-statistics.service.gov.uk/find-statistics/education-provision-children-under-5

DfE. (2015a). Effective school partnerships and collaboration for school improvement: A review of the evidence. Accessed 12th December 2022. https://assets.publishing.service.gov.uk/government/uploads/system/uploads/attachment_data/file/467855/DFE-RR466_-_School_improvement_effective_school_partnerships.pdf

DfE. 2010. Practitioners' experience of the early years foundation stage. Accessed 12th January 2023. https://assets.publishing.service.gov.uk/government/uploads/system/uploads/attachment_data/file/181479/DFE-RR029.pdf

DfE. (2015b). Special educational needs and disability code of practice: 0 to 25 years. Accessed 10th January 2023. https://assets.publishing.service.gov.uk/government/uploads/system/uploads/attachment_data/file/398815/SEND_Code_of_Practice_January_2015.pdf

Education Endowment Foundation. (2020). Special educational needs in mainstream schools: Evidence review. Accessed 22nd August 2022. https://educationendowmentfoundation.org.uk/public/files/Publications/Send/EEF_SEND_Evidence_Review.pdf

Goodall, J. (2017). *Narrowing the Achievement Gap: Parental Engagement with Children's Learning.* London: Routledge.

Hamilton, P. (2013). Fostering effective and sustainable home-school relations with migrant worker parents: A new story to tell? *International Studies in Sociology of Education*, 23(4), pp. 298–317.

James, C. 2007. Collaborative practice: The basis of good educational work. *Management in Education*, 21(4). DOI: 10.1177/0892020607082674

Lamb, B. (2009). Lamb inquiry review of SEN and disability information. Accessed 2nd September 2022. https://dera.ioe.ac.uk/9042/1/Lamb%20Inquiry%20Review%20of%20SEN%20and%20Disability%20Information.pdf

Parentkind. (2022). Involvement in school life. Accessed 19th November 2022. https://www.parentkind.org.uk/for-parents/home-and-school/involvement-in-school-life

National College for Teaching and Leadership. (2014). Freedom to lead: A study of outstanding primary school leadership in England. Accessed 15th May 2022. https://assets.publishing.service.gov.uk/government/uploads/system/uploads/attachment_data/file/363794/RR374A_-_Outstanding_primaries_final_report.pdf

Roberts, J. and Simpson, K. (2016). A review of research into stakeholder perspectives on inclusion of students with autism in mainstream schools. *International Journal of Inclusive Education*, 20(10). Doi:10.1080/13603116.2016.1145267

The Convention on the Rights of the Child. (1990). Accessed 9th July 2023. https://www.unicef.org/wpcontent/uploads/2010/05/UNCRC_united_nations_convention_on_the_rights_of_the_child.pdf

4 Voluntary action

Alison Body

Introduction

Do you remember the last time you were asked to donate to a school fundraiser? Maybe it was through baking a cake for the school fair, a Parent Teacher Association (PTA) charity quiz fundraiser, a sponsored activity, or simply in response to a direct ask for help? Perhaps as a parent you volunteer your time as a school governor, listen to children read or run an after-school activity? And if you are a teacher, when was the last time you dipped into your funds to buy resources for your pupils or teaching? Or when did you last rope family or friends into helping to change or decorate your classroom or outside space? When we reflect on these activities, we quickly realise voluntary action is an important and multi-layered part of everyday school life with a combination of parents, grandparents, community members, teachers (and their friends and families!) and children coming together to raise funds and partake in voluntary action for the good of the entire school community.

Such activity enables schools to draw upon a wide range of additional skills and resources, can strengthen a school community and engage children in philanthropic activity from an early age. Thus, unsurprisingly, voluntary action in education tends to be viewed as a positive and good thing and is increasingly encouraged within policy and practice. Volunteering and fundraising in primary schools are becoming progressively central to school activities, with many primary schools keenly seeking to strategically engage and grow this area of activity. Schools increasingly purposefully foster engagement of volunteers to help increase teacher capacity, support children through one-to-one activities and provide additional resources for both core and extra-curricular activities.

Nonetheless, there are downsides. Here in the UK and further afield research highlights that this volunteering and fundraising activity is not unproblematic. Having conducted extensive research into this topic I and colleagues look at this issue from a UK perspective. Our research shows that schools in more wealthy areas can raise substantially more than those in poorer areas (Body et al., 2017; Body & Hogg, 2021). The result of this is that schools in more socio-economically advantaged areas will have more per head to spend on their pupils than schools in less socio-economically advantaged areas (Body et al., 2017; Body & Hogg, 2021). This comes against the backdrop of concerns about school funding, which continues to be one of the most discussed topics in education over the past few years. Increasingly, schools have been looking for ways in which they can squeeze as much as possible out of their existing budgets and raise more funds to boost those budgets further. In doing so, many have looked to voluntary donations of time and money as a solution, engaging parents, children and the community in a range of activities, many of which can be enjoyable.

In this chapter I draw together the extensive research carried out by myself and my colleagues into the role of voluntary action in education, to present a series potential concerns, possibilities and lessons learnt, which may be of benefit to both schools and the wider community in developing voluntary action in primary schools which embraces and supports the whole-school community.

Why do schools seek to attract voluntary action?

Schools face a significant set of challenges, including recruitment and retention problems, funding woes and ever-increasing pressure to improve performance. Unsurprisingly, schools increasingly turn to additional sources of support from volunteers and fundraised income in trying to counter these challenges. Indeed, my own research highlights that the primary motivation for schools engaging and seeking to increase voluntary action are funding challenges. It is difficult to get to the bottom of the funding crisis in education. For several years, schools have been campaigning that they do not have enough funding, whilst the Department for Education continuously repeat the claim that they are funding education more than ever before. In fact, both claims are true, if not rather misleading on the part of the Department for Education.

According to the Institute of Fiscal Studies (Farquharson et al., 2021), spending on education makes up the second-largest element of public sector spending in the UK, behind only health. In 2020–21, for example, it represented about £99 billion in today's prices, which is about 4.5% of national income. However, between 2009–10 and 2019–20, school spending per pupil in England fell by 9% in real terms, representing the largest cut in over 40 years.

The COVID-19 pandemic outbreak in 2020 exacerbated the funding issues as schools and teachers quickly had to move teaching online whilst simultaneously supporting the children of key workers and those at risk within the school setting. Resources continued to be put under pressure under the 'COVID catch-up'. The 2021 Spending Review included an extra £4.4 billion for the schools budget in 2024–25 as compared with previous plans. This is a good start as it should likely reverse the 9% cuts from 2009–10 to 2019–20. However, this is not quite as good at it may seem as, when combined with the current spending plans (at time of writing), the Institute of Fiscal Studies project that spending per pupil in 2024 will only return to about the same level as in 2010. This means that over a period of 15 years there will have been no overall growth in schools spending, a situation which is unprecedented since the launch of the Education Act in the 1900s.

What teachers say:

"We couldn't keep some of our more vulnerable children in school without the support the volunteers give, we simply don't have the staff."

"I am very angry that this is the focus of schools, to keep heads above water and not on providing excellent education."

"Volunteers are a massive cost saving for us, we've had to let most of our support staff go, and we've actively replaced them with volunteers – it's not right but it is necessary given the budget constraints we face."

Most worryingly, deprived schools have seen the largest cuts over the last decade. For example, the most deprived secondary schools saw a 14% real-terms fall in spending per pupil between 2009–10 and 2019–20, compared with a 9% drop for the least-deprived schools. Furthermore, private school fees increased by 23% over the same period of time, significantly increasing the gap between funds spent on the children from the wealthiest backgrounds and those spent on the poorest; and, finally, 'the National Funding Formula has continued this pattern by providing bigger real-terms increases for the least deprived schools (8–9%) than for the most deprived ones (5%) between 2017–18 and 2022–23' (Farquharson et al., 2021: p. 27).

Within this context school budgets continued to be squeezed as demand for support rises, from teachers' wages, to school running costs and increased facility costs. At the same time, community support services have been slashed over the past decade, placing increased pressure on schools to meet children's and families' increased support needs. Thus, as the National Funding Formula leaves the majority of schools even worse off than previously, particularly those in deprived areas, demand for Pupil Premium increases and community support decreases, it is unsurprising that schools are placing a greater emphasis on charitable and voluntary action as a means of boosting school budgets and providing additional resources (Body, 2020).

Fundraising

In the context of this study the term fundraising refers to activities and donated income which is raised and used to directly contribute towards school activities and support for the school community, rather than fundraising for wider causes such as BBC Children in Need or Comic Relief. This activity also includes the role of the Parent Teacher Association (PTA), and philanthropic partnerships and collaborations which the school forms with third sector and corporate partners. Unlike volunteering, schools' approaches to fundraising tend to be slightly more erratic in nature; however, fundraising appears to be increasingly more central to schools' activities. As one headteacher commented, *"unfortunately, in this financial climate, it is now necessary to fundraise in order to enhance provision for children"*. However, recent research reveals that only around one-third of schools agree that fundraising forms a core part of their school business plan. In contrast around two-thirds of the schools said they were actively trying to increase their annual fundraising income. Fundraised income is used in schools to support both core statutory provision, as well as extra-curricular and additional support.

How do schools fundraise?

Primary schools draw upon a wide range of methods to raise funds, with more traditional methods such as school fairs, fun events, non-uniform days, competitions and raffles remaining as the most popular fundraising choices for schools. Increasingly, however, more schools are relying on asking for donations directly from parents, foundations, the local community and businesses. Indeed, over one-third of parents have been asked to donate to a school fund (ParentKind, 2021), whilst school applications to philanthropic funding pots increases (Body, 2020).

Schools primarily raise funds primarily to support the educational experiences of their children and to counter funding challenges. However, there are further additional benefits to fundraising, including bolstering community relationships, improving relationships with parents and carers, and providing educational opportunities for children to engage in, and lead, fundraising projects. When we spoke to schools about their fundraising efforts, they frequently acknowledged the power of good relationships with the whole community and use fundraising events as a way to foster such relationships.

> **What teachers say:**
>
> *"It teaches the children key skills about giving."*
> *"It's good for parental involvement."*
> *"These events do bring the community together which is essential to developing many aspects of schools in deprived areas."*

To achieve fundraising success, schools adopt a variety of strategically focused initiatives and, when successful, most commonly have individuals dedicated to the fundraising roles. Activities include a combination of internal and external activities, such as proactive engagement of volunteer fundraisers to raise funds within the local community; high-profile events run by the PTA; setting up parent funds to allow parents to regularly donate to the school; income-generating 'social enterprise'-type activities such as hiring out buildings; collaborative arrangements with private schools, such as sharing resources; sponsorship of donations from private businesses; and regular applications to charitable trusts and grant-making bodies, such as the National Lottery Fund.

Alongside proactively encouraging PTA activities, schools are increasingly employing individuals to lead on these fundraising activities or engaging the services of consultants. Alternatively, schools are investing in training for staff and volunteers to increase fundraising success.

Nonetheless, school leaders and teachers are increasingly recognising the growing financial pressures on families and thus they take efforts to poverty-proof schools, and question whether or not it is indeed ethical to approach families whose resources may already be stretched.

Thus, we are now seeing greater emphasis on 'going beyond the school gates', as schools turn to philanthropic foundations, corporate partners and grant-making bodies to increase philanthropic income.

> **Top tips from research and practice to increase individual donated income:**
>
> - Carefully consider your community.
> - Actively ask for support; do not simply expect them to come to you with money.
> - Take a holistic approach to fundraising by embedding it throughout school activities and throughout the year. People may not be able to give much in one go but may be happy to give a little now and then.
> - Invest time and resources in fundraising – it is not free or easy and you will need to invest to generate a return.
> - Think about what you want to raise money for and how best to appeal to individuals, corporate partners or funding bodies. When you ask for donations or support, tell people what their money will be spent on and the positive contribution their donation will make.

- Empower the school community and friends to fundraise on your behalf. Make sure they know why the school needs donations and how they can be made.
- Seize opportunities to raise the profile of your school's causes. The more people, groups and even businesses know why you need money, the more donations you will get.
- Make donating an easy process. For example, donation boxes at school and donation buttons on your website make giving straightforward.
- Thank all supporters promptly and sincerely. Donors who feel appreciated are far more likely to give to you again.
- Demonstrate and communicate the impact of your fundraising efforts. If donations paid for a trip, tell donors how that trip went. If they paid for improvements to the school, invite donors to come and see them. Make donors feel part of something special.

Challenges in achieving fundraising success

Research highlights that there is a general lack of knowledge and awareness about how to fundraise among school staff. This is perhaps unsurprising given that most people enter the education sector in order to support children and young people, rather than to fundraise for schools. Nonetheless, whilst most schools engage in more traditional fundraising activities such as school fêtes, fewer actively seek to fundraise from other sources such as philanthropists, charitable trusts or crowdfunding. The reasons for this are multi-faceted; some school staff suggest these were inappropriate activities for schools to engage in, whilst others feel that they did not know where to start or even what funding opportunities are available. Indeed, where fundraising activity existed within schools, it tended to be around a particular individuals personal experience rather than a strategic approach, for example having a professional fundraiser as a governor.

What teachers say:

"We're lucky we have a fundraiser as a governor who has done loads for us, we wouldn't have done anything without her."

"Some schools do not have the parental/community support for fundraising. By engaging in this raising our own funds to bridge budgets we are giving the green light to the government agenda to corporatise education. I think we should be mindful of how much money we are asking parents for, especially if in an area of 'economic deprivation'."

Furthermore, school staff highlight concerns about lacking the skills to actively fundraise and/or form charitable collaborative partnerships. This seems particularly apparent for fundraising activities such as bid-writing, approaching charitable trusts and engaging local business support. Where voluntary action has been successful in schools, it was, more often than not, grown from a grassroots perspective based upon the skills and/or interests of one or two individuals in the school; this presents a significant risk in that if or when these individuals move on from the school, so do their skills.

Another challenge faced by many is that the concept of fundraising in schools raises significant ideological contention between schools. Accepted as historical part of school life, school fairs, events and Parent Teacher Fundraising Association activities have long been considered to be appropriate and community engaging. However, many school staff reflect negatively on the growing necessity to seek to increase funds beyond these activities. Indeed, schools tend to fall into four overarching groupings with regards to this topic; survival, the ideologically opposed,; nicety; and the ideologically for.

Those focusing on **survival** reflect on the need to raise funds purely to support their school community. They often feel forced into the position and thus see fundraising as a transactional process, which can mean that wider community benefits are not experienced.

Schools who fell into the **ideologically opposed** shared strong concerns about reliance upon fundraising to support core activities. Viewing fundraising as a mechanism for bolstering inadequate funding, some felt that seeking to increase funding through philanthropic income generation supports the corporatisation and marketisation of education to which they were ideologically opposed. Here there is a strong feeling that funding should predominantly come from government and as such leadership in the school does not support growing this area of activity.

Equally, schools who saw fundraising as an **added nicety** sought to use fundraising as a community engagement activity and did not wish to pursue this further. Schools also expressed concern over fundraising from parents, raising worries about the socio-economic position of families, lack of community support and fear of alienating parents and the local community. Indeed, research highlights that increasingly habitual activities such as non-school uniform days and dressing-up days are problematic and exclusionary for many families facing poverty (Mazzoli Smith & Todd, 2016). In short, some children and families can afford to participate in fundraising activities as easily as others, and this must be taken into consideration in any schools fundraising efforts (Body et al., 2023).

Finally, some schools are **ideologically for** fundraising in education, viewing this activity as a way to make their school stand out. Interestingly, schools attracting significant amounts of voluntary action appear to accept the potential inequalities this brings, arguing that voluntary action is a way for schools in wealthier areas to 'balance out pupil premium advantage'. However, this argument is undermined by the evidence. Schools in wealthier areas by no means have a monopoly on seeking to engage more voluntary action, nor do they have a monopoly on using a wide range of activities to do so. Rather, while efforts to increase voluntary action are relatively evenly spread across schools regardless of the relative wealth of the area in which they are located, schools in wealthier areas are rewarded with greater fundraising and volunteer recruitment success than schools in areas of disadvantage.

Engaging volunteers

> **What teachers say:**
>
> *"Volunteers help to develop a sense of community beyond the school gates."*
> *"Volunteers bring a wealth of knowledge, skills and experience which enriches the lives of our students."*
> *"Volunteers bring a wealth of experience and talent to the school."*

Volunteers play an important role in primary education. Setting aside the important role of governors as volunteers and their duty of governance in education settings, we instead here focus on volunteer activities within school life. Almost all primary schools engage volunteers within their day-to-day activities in one way or another. In turn, volunteers are valued by schools and seen as an important and central component within the school workforce. Indeed, our research highlighted that 93% of schools say volunteers form an important part of their school community, with 73% of schools reporting that they would like to increase the number of volunteers they have, and 52% stating that they would also like to increase the number of hours their current volunteers give (Body et al., 2017). Nonetheless, only around one-third of schools reported finding it easy to draw in volunteers, leaving the remaining two-thirds of schools struggling to attract the volunteer support they would ideally like. Schools in areas of higher economic deprivation were more likely to report struggling to engage volunteers.

***Who Volunteers*:** whilst unsurprisingly volunteering in education dropped dramatically during the COVID-19 pandemic, pre-pandemic research shows that over five million individuals were involved in voluntary activity within schools in the UK. Unsurprisingly, the schools report parents of children currently at the school as the most likely group to volunteer, with 96% of schools engaging this group of volunteers. Almost two-thirds of schools report engaging the individuals from the local community, whilst approximately one-third of schools engage the grandparents and extended family of current pupils. Members of staff also make up an interesting group of potential volunteers. Just over 30% of schools identified as volunteers, doing activities which were outside of their working hours and contractual obligations. Furthermore, 25% of schools engaged family and friends of staff as volunteers. A much smaller proportion of schools engaged parents who had formerly had children at the school as volunteers, suggesting that once a child moves on from a school so does the parents' commitment as a volunteer to that school.

***What do Volunteers Do*:** Volunteers engage in a wide range of activities to support primary schools, from educational provision, supporting fundraising activities and trips, to general maintenance of the school. Furthermore, different activities attract different volunteers, with some volunteers giving time on a regular basis (once a month or more) and others supporting the school more sporadically with specific tasks or activities. For example, female volunteers are more likely to volunteer regularly, that is more than once a month, within the classroom; whilst male volunteers are more likely to sporadically volunteer and engage in maintenance and one-off activities, such as the creation of a new garden area. Furthermore, sporadic volunteers, that is those who volunteer less than once a month, perhaps unsurprisingly, were more likely to support with fundraising activities for the school, as well as events, trips and educational visits and general maintenance of the school. These are all activities which may occur once a term or annually and are therefore more attractive to those only able or willing to make a smaller and potentially less formal commitment.

Benefits of engaging volunteers

Accepting that parents of children within the school form the vast majority of school volunteers, teachers identify four main benefits of engaging volunteers within school settings.

What teachers say:

"They [volunteers] free up teaching staff to do their core jobs."

"Volunteers can provide support for reading which staff do not have the time to provide."

"Volunteer support improves the ratio of adult to child so that teachers can get on with teaching the curriculum."

Volunteers as support for teachers: Appropriately skilled volunteers can provide much-needed additional support within the classroom. Considering volunteers as a practical resource for the school brings dual benefits. First, volunteers can practically reduce pressure on teachers in the classroom by supporting educational activities, such as art-based activities and group work, or extra-curricular activities. Second, volunteers can deliver one-to-one support to children around a particular need, for example listening to reading or supporting writing development. In short, volunteers can bring an array of different skills and expertise to supplement and support teaching and extra-curricular activities.

Volunteers as role models and support for children: Volunteers can act as positive role models and provide emotional wellbeing support for children. Teachers highlight this as particularly important for those children who are perceived as perhaps not having as much support within their home environment as others may have. Here teachers identify this additional capacity as an opportunity to provide supplementary one-on-one support for more vulnerable children and provide children with positive role models.

What teachers say:

"If volunteers are professional, committed and have high expectations for themselves and the children, they provide children with excellent role models."

"The use of volunteers gives children additional opportunities to practice skills that they find difficult or challenging."

"Volunteers can bring additional skills and support to those children who don't get support at home."

Volunteers as links to the wider community: Volunteers provide valuable links to the local community. Teachers associate this benefit as having both an internal purpose, supporting the school, and an external purpose in terms of 'reaching out' to the local community. This benefit is twofold; first, strengthening the role of the school as a community hub, and second, acting as a conduit to attract more local support into the school.

What teachers say:

"There is an increased community awareness of what happens at the school."

"Volunteers add to the family and community feel in our school, which matches well with our school values of caring for one another."

"The school is the hub of the community, by using volunteers we strengthen these links."

88 Voluntary action

Volunteers as free resource: The fourth and final benefit identified by teachers is the view of volunteers as an 'additional' financial resource for schools. This framing of volunteers as a financial benefit recognises the wider contribution volunteers make to the school community considering the strain on school budgets. Volunteers are seen as a mechanism within which to increase capacity and resources at a minimal cost to the school. This, of course, links to all of the previous strengths identified in this case, however, schools are very direct about volunteers having a direct financial benefit to the school.

What teachers say:

"Cost – being able to deliver additional support activities without is putting strain on already stretched school budgets."

"They are an additional resource and bring a wealth of skills to the school."

"It gives us the ability to organise and provide additional special events and fundraising at minimal cost."

Top tips from research and practice on successfully engaging volunteers

- Take a whole-school approach. Though it is recommended one person be given the time and capacity to manage volunteers, the whole-school team has to be on board to really maximise the benefits. Your governors, teachers and pupils are your best recruiters of volunteers so make sure they are aware of the value volunteers can add.
- Think about who is most likely to volunteer and actively seek to recruit these people. Most volunteers will do so because they have a vested or personal interested in the cause; in this case they will often have a child at the school either currently or they may have had one there in the past.
- Ask individuals in the right way and do not always wait for people to approach you; think about how you can proactively engage individuals and why they may want to help. Again, it can be anyone involved with the school that makes the ask.
- Be very clear about what your expectations are and clearly communicate these to your volunteers. Make sure you understand their expectations and support these as much as you can, but also be clear when you cannot meet these expectations.
- Once you are clear about what you want volunteers to do, give them the training and support them to do it. Ensure you provide ongoing support for them to do it and that volunteers know who to ask for help.
- Thank volunteers regularly and meaningfully. This does not need to be any more than a simple 'thank you', but it could also include cards at Christmas, invitations to events or anything else you or your pupils can think of.

Challenges in engaging volunteers

Engaging volunteers isn't always easy and schools identify several factors to take into consideration when preparing to engage volunteers. It takes time and resources to engage, train, coordinate and manage volunteers within a school. Too often, volunteer recruitment and management is an add-on to a member of staff's role and is not given full consideration. Volunteers require training and support, just like any other member of staff in the school, and this requires some investment of resources, including time, training and management. Furthermore, there are bureaucratic aspects, such as applying for Disclosure and Barring Service (DBS) checks, which can be costly and time-consuming.

Drawing on schools' experiences of engaging volunteers, several more challenges emerge. For example, individual volunteers' time constraints are seen as a limiting factor by schools, alongside their ability to make regular commitments. Ideally, schools want volunteers who would provide support at a regular time each week, and who could develop long-term relationships with specific staff and children. Where this was not the case, schools raise concerns about the consistency of support. There are also several issues in engaging parents and carers which require consideration. Schools acknowledge potential conflicts of interest in parental motivations as volunteers and raised concerns around confidentiality and accountability between parents. Therefore, schools have to be careful in terms of where volunteers are allocated in the school, especially when engaging parents, and ensure all aspects of confidentiality are adhered to by volunteers.

> **What teachers say:**
>
> *"Good intentions are not enough in times of heightened accountability."*
>
> *"Ensuring that the volunteers are correctly skilled for the role that we wish them to takes time. Many need some form of training to do what we want them to well enough to support the learning of the children."*
>
> *"With challenging children there is a need for risk assessing the health and safety of volunteers."*

Wider social issues, policy shifts and curriculum changes also pose challenges for the engagement of volunteers in schools. Ongoing wider societal shifts and policy changes contribute to the creation of barriers in engaging volunteers. Schools, particularly those in perceived areas of disadvantage, highlight challenges in engaging volunteers from cohorts of parents with their own negative experiences of school, and thus they can be harder to engage in positively contributing to school life. Furthermore, some schools perceive a sense of general apathy by parents towards the education of their children and a general unwillingness to engage. Wider societal pressures also mean families face increasing workloads and a lack of available time to volunteer was also recognised as a challenge. Furthermore, shifts in social policy concerning the school curriculum and education also pose significant barriers in terms of volunteers training needs and skill development.

> **What teachers say:**
>
> *"Volunteers cannot keep up with curriculum changes."*
>
> *"It is getting harder and harder to get parents to offer their help – even those that we know do not work or are able to help don't come forwards when we appeal."*
>
> *"Some hard-to-reach parents are scared of school."*

A wicked problem?

Here we consider voluntary action in education as a 'wicked problem', meaning that it is contradictory in nature, with no clear answers. Whilst we recognise the many benefits volunteering and fundraising can bring to schools, we also recognise a significant issue in the fact that this activity is not evenly spread across schools, with some schools significantly benefiting more than others. This means that voluntary action can be seen as compounding inequality in education. Even more worryingly, my own and colleagues' recent research highlights that these inequalities are increasing as we face a continued hyper-marketisation of education (Body & Hogg, 2021).

For starters, we know that voluntary action in education is increasing. This is true in terms of donations of both money and time. Regarding the former, the amount schools raise on average has risen from £41 per pupil per year in 2016 to £51 per pupil per year in 2018; this increases to £94 per pupil when we consider PTA income. For the latter, the amount of volunteer time schools receive has increased from 12.5 minutes per pupil per week in 2016 to 21 minutes per pupil per week in 2018. Schools have achieved these increases through a more strategic focus on targeting their fundraising activities on less traditional sources such as businesses or foundations, and by taking a whole-school approach to volunteer recruitment (Body & Hogg, 2021).

What teachers say:

"Voluntary action is a necessity to bridge the gap and the decreasing funding we are receiving… But is this something we really want our schools to be focusing on? Surely they should be focused on the education and development of our children. Our backs are against the wall – it looks like we will increasingly have to do this, but it is not a teacher's core skillset and arguably it shouldn't have to be."

"Volunteers are a massive cost saving for us, we've had to let most of our support staff go, and we've actively replaced them with volunteers – it's not right but it is necessary given the budget constraints we face."

Nonetheless, this increase in voluntary action in schools is not evenly dispersed. Instead, we are seeing several breakaway schools with a strong culture of philanthropy embedded throughout the school, which are moving significantly ahead of the other schools in terms of voluntary action. A culture of philanthropy means ensuring that the wider school community are aware of the benefits of voluntary action and what requirements the school has, and this is essential – although not enough on its own – for schools to break away. The highest fundraising schools raised nearly £600 per pupil per year in 2018, more than doubling the highest figure of £250 per pupil per year in 2016. Put simply, a large proportion of fundraised income is concentrated in a few schools – the top 10% of these schools account for 25% of all the donated income, and the top 1% of schools account for 10% of all the donated income to primary schools. If we translate this into figures, in the 2018 research the top 1% of the schools by fundraised collectively raised £476,784, compared to a total of fundraised income of £875 for the bottom 1%. In terms of the amount raised per pupil, this means the top 1% of fundraising schools bring in £593 of additional income per child through donations, whereas the bottom 1% secured only £0.33 per child per year of additional income (Body & Hogg, 2021).

Thus, our research shows that the gaps between schools in terms of voluntary action success are widening (Body et al., 2023). While some schools break away, others are standing still. Most notably, this gap reflects existing patterns of deprivation. Schools in the wealthier half of areas attract over twice as much in terms of donations in both money and time as schools in the more deprived half of areas. While embracing a culture of philanthropy has benefits for all schools, those in wealthier areas benefit far more, further amplifying inequalities in education.

Finally, research shows that the push to attract more voluntary action is brought about by necessity rather than choice. The proportion of schools who said they were reliant on fundraised income to deliver core statutory education (day-to-day teaching activities) provision rose from 28% in 2016 to 43% in 2018, while the proportion of schools who rely on fundraised income to deliver general school activities (wider curriculum-enhancing provision) has risen from 52% in 2016 to 75% in 2018. This increase reflects a troubling trend in school funding, with budget pressures forcing schools to explore alternative funding sources.

So whilst there are lots of benefits of voluntary action to celebrate the growth in voluntary action, the problem remains wicked as we identify that the driver behind these efforts is declining budgets due to decreased statutory funding, and increased budgetary spending pressures; we are seeing a growing gulf between those schools who can access significant resources of time and treasure in the communities and those who cannot; and schools are increasingly having to do more than just educate. They are increasingly raising money and recruiting to provide social welfare support for pupils and the wider community. This should raise concern with educators because as this escalates, inequalities will grow, and the concern is that schools will become privatised by stealth.

Is there a winning formula?

Although we know the socio-economic context is important, it is not the only factor. Indeed, many schools from deprived areas demonstrate significant fundraising and volunteer engagement success, but such success does not occur without a concerted effort. Summarising my previous research on this topic (Body, 2017) and drawing on the evidence presented in this chapter, here I present the distinctive characteristics and/or actions schools, working in all areas, can take forwards to achieve voluntary action success. In short, schools who are particularly successful at attracting volunteers and fundraised income demonstrated a proactive approach to voluntary action, embracing a culture of philanthropy.

Schools should adopt a proactive approach: For schools to achieve success they need to proactively engage in fundraising and volunteer management: this means having strategic and operational commitment across the school.

This is achieved in four ways:

- First, as almost all donations and commitments to volunteer occur as a response to someone being asked, for schools to achieve increased voluntary action they must proactively and directly ask donors and volunteers for support (Wiepking & Maas, 2009). It is important schools also think about moving 'beyond the school gate' in this ask, not solely focusing on parents and local members of the community, especially if those individuals' resources are already stretched. Instead, schools should explore other opportunities such as working in partnership with charities, applying for funds from foundations and engaging corporate support from businesses.

- Second, schools should be specific in this ask. By facilitating donors and volunteers to donate their money and time to specific projects or activities, for example creating a new community garden project or re-stocking the school library, schools are likely to attract increased amounts of voluntary action. Furthermore, being specific in asking volunteers to donate their time to a particular activity, such as reading with children, clearly outlines expectations for volunteers and is likely to increase long-term commitment.
- Third, though fundraising and volunteer recruitment may be centrally coordinated by one or few individuals, it should not be the sole responsibility of that one individual within the school or the PTA. Instead, fundraising and volunteer management should be a collective response supported by the whole school and engages all members of the school community as much as possible, including the governing body, parents and children.
- Fourth, for schools to maximise their fundraised income and volunteer engagement they need to maximise existing opportunities, as well as seeking new ones. In doing so, schools can look to explore a range of fundraising approaches (i.e. individual donors, events, charitable trusts, corporate partners, etc.) and tailor the ways they ask for donations of time and money to suit the school and local community needs.

Creating a Philanthropic Narrative: Closely tied to taking a proactive approach to voluntary action, creating a positive narrative for why a school should engage in this activity is necessary in terms of attracting funds and volunteers. This is important, both internally to the school and externally with partners. Internally, schools need to celebrate and acknowledge their fundraising and volunteer successes. Highlighting these successes supports the development of a culture of philanthropy across the school. Rather than frame their story in the context of depleting budgets, schools can consider how additional funding is used to go above and beyond statutory funding obligations.

Investing in People and Skills: Though schools wish to increase their fundraised income and volunteer support, they often feel inhibited to fully pursue this due to a lack of time, skills and knowledge. Therefore, successful fundraising and volunteer recruitment and retention attempts tended to be grown out of existing opportunities from within the current structure of the school, generally as an 'add-on' to an individual's existing role. To maximise these opportunities and identify additional new opportunities, schools need to consider how to equip individuals tasked with fundraising and volunteer management with the appropriate time, skills and knowledge, alongside supporting a wider understanding of fundraising and volunteer management across the school to ensure that the role of voluntary action is understood and that expectations remain realistic.

Identifying Dual Benefits: Schools are better placed to secure increased fundraising income and volunteer time when the school is at the heart of the community, and voluntary action is able to have a 'dual benefit', meeting both educational and community needs. Cuts to public and voluntary sector providers are placing increased pressure on schools as wider community support for children and young people diminishes. Schools fundraising and volunteer engagement efforts can be used to readdress these issues, for example providing early intervention and emotional wellbeing support, resulting in schools occupying positions both in education and social welfare provision. Working collaboratively in partnership with local charities supports such initiatives. This dual benefit, if clearly articulated, can encourage donors and volunteers to give more.

Conclusion

This chapter has attempted to begin to expand the discussion concerning fundraising and volunteering in education. In doing so, we consider the benefits and barriers of fundraising and engaging volunteers to support education. Parents, teachers, children and the local community members all make positive contributions to schools' voluntary action efforts. Nonetheless, we also recognise the ideological contention and issues which rise from the increased pressure on schools to find alternative sources of funding in response to depleting budgets, and the increased pressure felt by schools due to cuts in community-based support services. Thus, it also attempts to understand the pragmatic solutions that schools can pursue in responding to these challenges. By engaging in recognised good practice, such as being proactive in their approaches to fundraising, creating a philanthropic narrative, investing in people and skills, and identifying dual benefits, schools can achieve fundraising and volunteer success. Furthermore, by drawing on both the good practice and challenges faced, we can attempt to identify "what works" for schools trying to increase their fundraised income and volunteer support.

On a final note, primary schools value voluntary action. Both volunteering and philanthropic support make positive contributions to a school's capacity to deliver core and extra-curricular activity. Voluntary action in whichever form supports the breadth of delivery and contributes to positive relationships with parents and the wider community. However, the increasing blurring of the roles of the private, public and voluntary sector, alongside the drive for the commodification of education raises significant questions about the reliance on voluntary action as a mechanism to support primary schools into the future.

References

Body, A. (2017). Fundraising for primary schools in England—Moving beyond the school gates. *International Journal of Nonprofit and Voluntary Sector Marketing*, 22(4), p. e1582.

Body, A. (2020). *Children's Charities in Crisis: Early Intervention and the State*. Bristol: Policy Press.

Body, A. and Hogg, E. (2021). Collective co-production in English public services: The case of voluntary action in primary education. *Voluntary Sector Review*, 13(2), pp. 243–259.

Body, A., Holman, K. and Hogg, E. (2017). To bridge the gap? Voluntary action in primary schools. *Voluntary Sector Review*, 8(3), pp. 251–271.

Body, A., Lau, E., Cameron, L. and Cunliffe, J. (2023) *Educating for Social Good: Part 1 Mapping Children's Active Civic Learning in England*. Canterbury: University of Kent.

Farquharson, C., Sibieta, L., Tahir, I. and Waltmann, B. (2021). *2021 Annual Report on Education Spending in England*. London: Institute of Fiscal Studies.

Mazzoli Smith, L. and Todd, L. (2016). *Poverty proofing the school day: evaluation and development report*. Newcastle: Newcastle University.

ParentKind. (2021). *Parent Voice Report 2021*. ParentKind. Accessed 20th February 2022. https://www.parentkind.org.uk/uploads/files/1/Parent%20Voice%20Report%202021%20-%20In%20Full.pdf

Wiepking, P. and Maas, I. (2009). Resources that make you generous: Effects of social and human resources on charitable giving. *Social Forces*, 87(4), pp. 1973–1995.

5 Engaging the disengaged and overcoming barriers

Why is engagement important?

Having positive interactions with schools is important and can positively impact a child's education. Understanding the importance of this can influence educators' decisions and practise. Harris and Goodall (2007) identified parental engagement as a key component to children's academic success.

As society changes and increasing demands become a common entity in our everyday lives, relationships can become one of the factors to suffer. However, our understanding around the importance of meaningful relationships between home and school, and the vital role both play in a child's life, continues to grow.

Research by the Education Endowment Foundation (2021a) identified the importance of implementing consistent parental engagement initiatives in schools, and how an initiative with minimal costs can have such a powerful impact, 'Parental engagement has a positive impact on average of 4 months additional progress. It is crucial to consider how to engage with all parents to avoid widening attainment gaps.'

What does hard-to-reach mean?

The term 'hard-to-reach' can be used to describe families or parents who do not actively engage with schools or services associated with their children. Whilst the term may interpret distant families who are not interested in engaging, it may more often be the case that schools have not found an effective way to communicate with these specific families.

By creating a culture where parents play an active role within the school, such as a Parent Council, the hard-to-reach families become easier to connect with and, subsequently, become a vital pillar of support to their child.

In 'Engaging Parents in Raising Achievement: Do Parents Know They Matter?' by Harris and Goodall (2007) it states, 'It is clear that parents and students are in broad agreement about the value of parental engagement in the learning of young people'. The importance of relationship building and understanding the whole-school community is key to a school's success, as is the need to embed the principle as early as possible. Goodall (2012) identifies the need for early intervention for the sake of successful outcomes, 'begin engagement early, take an active (rather than passive or reactive) interest in the child's learning'.

If we are to analyse school and families on an equal measure, as we venture towards an equally collaborative approach, it begs the question – Is it the school that is hard to reach, or the families?

Within the school walls and the undisputed busy lives of the teachers and staff, the world of teaching and education fills the space. Every corridor, classroom and staffroom is filled with learning examples, plans, prospectus and academia. Practical lessons, engaging topics and wonderful learning takes place for 190 days or 6,175 hours an (academic) year. Yet for many parents, they spend most of their time mainly in the playground during drop-off and pick-up. The time, on average, that parents collectively spend time within the school each year includes; two parents' evenings (average 20 minutes each), book look twice a year (average 30 minutes each) and a Christmas nativity (approximately 45 minutes). Collectively, this means parents are spending an average of 2 hours and 25 minutes within the school a year, actively engaged in activities in conjunction with the teaching staff.

Of course, many schools invite parents to additional events: religious celebrations, assemblies, sports days etc. However, schools choose to come together with their families for these events and families are not necessarily communicating closely with staff, rather than attending as a spectator. Within this example, a common narrative remains – 'You are invited to attend…'. This means that the school manages the contact and the situation.

Engaging the disengaged

The very term itself, 'disengaged', suggests negativity and refusal. This chapter will look at some of the wider reasons and influences for disengagement and the impact that this can have on our children, families, school and community.

Whilst it is easy to presume that disengagement is a negative response to collaboration. It is important to remember that disengagement can manifest itself in many forms, leading educators to work as detectives, identifying strategies to overcome barriers and adapt new practice opportunities to work with families.

Barriers to engagement

These can include:

- Feeling intimidated by educational settings and staff;
- Challenging family circumstances;
- Being a carer for a family member;
- Financial difficulties;
- Mental health, physical health and wellbeing;
- Time constraints;
- Unsociable working hours;
- Families that struggle to articulate their needs;
- Communication and language barriers;
- Cultural and social background.

Kirsten Terry (Kent SEND Centre), shares her experience of engaging with disengaged families, specifically within SEND.

Kirsten Terry (Kent SEND, Shepway Tutoring and Free Parent Support Group)

"Engaging the disengaged" – somehow these words almost seem to be a barrier themselves. What does disengaged mean to you? Disinterested? Disconnected? Dissatisfied? Dispassionate? Distrustful? Disheartened? Just as we make judgements about the children in our classes, so do we make judgements about their parents. Yet, whereas the judgements we make about the children in our classes may be based on many pieces of evidence, can the same be said about the judgements we make about their parents? I am sure we have all heard comments about "that parent"; indeed, many of the parents I now work with are in fear of becoming "that parent" to their child's school.

The term "disengaged" may conjure up negative associations, a "them and us" situation where someone must take the blame for this lack of relationship between school and parent; however, we can think about this in a more positive way. Instead of apportioning blame, we can take responsibility for building relationships and encouraging engagement and positive dialogue between education professionals and parents so that the outcomes for the children we all care about can be improved.

I recently asked a group of parents of children with SEND how they felt about engaging with their schools. Among the words they used were 'dread', 'deflated', 'intimidated', 'misunderstood' and 'anxious'. One parent, whose child had recently moved school, explained that she had previously felt frustrated when trying to engage, but at the new school, her feelings had changed to being 'listened to' and 'understood'. To me, this shows that even though the relationship between school and parent can be difficult and there are barriers to overcome, this can be achieved. No parent should be written off and labelled as "that parent".

In order to overcome these barriers and "engage the disengaged", we must first consider the reasons why parents may not be engaging with the school. In some circumstances the cause may be more complex than others, but from my experience of talking and working with parents, some common reasons are:

- Feeling intimidated
- Previous bad experiences as a parent
- Negative experiences of education when they were a pupil
- Historic familial disengagement
- Unsociable working hours or working hours in general
- Fear
- Accessibility – parents with SEND or those with low literacy levels
- Poverty
- Cultural and/or religious reasons

I have worked with parents for whom the thought of sitting in front of their child's teacher's desk filled them with fear. They were transported back to their own childhood experiences and felt intimidated by the thought of the perceived "power differential" between them as the parent and the class teacher as the professional. On another occasion, I heard from a parent who was deaf and struggling to engage with her daughter's school because they rang her continually to discuss her child rather than engaging by text or email as she had requested.

Some of these 'barriers' may take longer to overcome than others, but that does not mean they are insurmountable. If we come from a belief that parental engagement is a key factor in providing the best educational experience for our children, if we place high importance and value on parental involvement in our schools then we can find ways to break down these barriers and create positive dialogue around the parent/school relationship for all parents.

When working as a class teacher, I always felt I was not only working with a child but their parents and family too. I recognised the importance of creating positive relationships – I didn't always get it right, but I tried my best to engage with the parents of every child in my class. This may seem like a lot of additional work for professionals already stretched to their limits; however, because I was lucky enough to work in a school with a strong ethos of parental involvement, I found it was manageable. I saw the positive results. It is very important that parental engagement is seen as a whole-school approach and not just the responsibility of individual teachers or the family liaison officer.

When developing an approach to increase the engagement of parents who may not normally engage it is important to replace terms such as "tricky parent" or "that parent" with positive language. Speaking positively about all parents in the staffroom, in staff meetings and, in general, will create a more constructive atmosphere around parental interaction. In addition, to this, there are a number of thought processes I have employed to grow relationships with parents who have previously been disengaged:

- Be open to engage
- Actively listen
- Acknowledge the parent's feelings even if that is difficult or uncomfortable
- Value the parent and their opinions
- Be consistent
- Be honest
- Be non-judgemental
- Be human – don't portray a role, be yourself

As a school, it is crucial that the whole-school community believes in the benefits of developing and maintaining parent–school relationships. Make sure your communication and interaction with parents is inclusive and accessible for all.

In addition:

- Believe in your parents and in their love for their child. With many different parenting styles it is easy to be critical or judgemental of a parent who does not do things "as we would do them." Societal factors and pressures can play a huge role in how a person may parent their child but in order to engage with all parents, it is necessary to push any prejudice aside and focus on the common goal – what will best help the child.
- Find out about the interests and realities of the parents in your school. What are the things that are important to your parents? What are the things that they struggle with on a day to day basis? In short – know your parents!

- Remember to communicate with parents for positive reasons. For some parents, the majority of their contact with school may be negative; for example, a parent whose child is struggling with their learning or behaviour. It is important in these cases that time is spent to talk to the parent and share positive news with them, however small. Working together and valuing the parent's interactions may positively impact on the child.
- Invite parents into school. This may seem to be a very obvious solution when trying to improve parental engagement and overcome barriers. Some schools will already do this to some extent, with parents' evenings, class assemblies and sports days for example. For some parents, these events may feel threatening and uncomfortable. Creating opportunities for events that are non-threatening and support the parent/child/school relationship, such as shared reading, art, history or cooking sessions, can help schools build trust and develop community. Parent Councils, like school councils, also give parents a true voice within the school and have a different purpose to the PTFA or school parent governors.
- Give them time. Parental engagement cannot be solved in a short period of time. Like any relationship, it will develop, change and have its ups and down. Given time, with a well-planned and dedicated approach, it can improve so trusting, respectful and mutually beneficial engagement becomes the norm.

To conclude, for some education professionals, parental engagement and increased parent contact can sometimes feel like a difficult and worrying path to travel. Our schools are judged, we are judged, our children are judged. For some, the continual criticism means that the doors are shut and remain firmly so with no more interaction than is expected or required. "We are the professionals – what can parents know?" From my experience, a school that involves its parents, listens to them, works alongside them and values them is a happy and positive place. Just as parents will fight to support their children, given the chance, they will do the same for their child's school. How do we engage those that are hard to reach? As we work with our children to identify their individual needs, trying different strategies to support the individual – so we should work with the individual needs of our parents in the same way. The rewards and feelings of community, family and unity are definitely worth it.

Mental health and wellbeing

The enormity and complexity of mental health can feel overwhelming, and leaders working to support their families, children and staff are no exception. Many of the key barriers listed can additionally result in poor mental health. In recent times, COVID-19 has been one of the main barriers to collaborative working. Whilst in many ways, new and inventive initiatives have developed, e.g. Zoom calls, online parents' evenings, online lessons, and socially distanced events. This has also led to gaps widening between face-to-face interactions and the 'presence' within the school building itself. Whilst for some, they accommodated and managed the change, this highlighted parents that may be more articulate and confident in communicating through methods such as online platforms and emails. Whilst for others, it contributed to the feeling of vulnerability and isolation. The responsibility to support children's learning at home, with many parents doing this for more than one child, whilst maintaining their own job role, became overwhelming, 'Having to provide home schooling while not feeling prepared and equipped for it, is likely to cause frustration amongst parents' (Parczewska, 2020). For parents that already felt judged by the education system, the barrier intensified.

> I tried my best to support my children during lockdown and I was not anxious at first about helping them with their work. The first lockdown wasn't too bad in terms of work and expectations. However, the second lockdown was much more difficult. I appreciated that the teachers had pressure on them to ensure the children were learning but as a parent, the increased responsibility was overwhelming. I noticed after a while that it was impacting my mental health, which was already struggling with the concerns linked to COVID. I felt like a failure to my children as I couldn't help them with their work all the time and I felt embarrassed to say to the teachers that I didn't understand my children's lessons. Even though I tried to reassure myself that I wouldn't be the only one going through this, I felt really isolated. Even after the schools went back, I worried that the other children would go back better equipped and ready to learn than my children would.
>
> Anonymous Mother

The aftermath of COVID left many schools reflecting on their practice, with many continuing to adopt new methods and approaches. Alex Wallace talks about reflective practice as a professional – an important tool for personal and professional self-improvement and how the shift in a school's culture, impacted on outcomes for the pupils, their families and staff.

> **Alex Wallace – Former Teacher and Content Producer for the Schools and Academies Show**
>
> All staff in schools genuinely want to do the best by their pupils and parents, that's why it hurts so much when we get it wrong. It can be difficult to reconcile your feelings when you walk away from an interaction thinking, "That could have gone better, I got that wrong." These feelings are only natural, but they can linger with you like a bad taste; that's only human and it's the sign of a practitioner who cares.
>
> Having taught in two very different primary schools but geographically very close, made me view the way we worked with parents and carers in a very different light. The school where I did my initial teacher training and started my teaching career was located in a leafy suburb of a non-descript city in the East Midlands. The intake has traditionally been affluent white middle-class pupils, many of whom went on to the fee-paying secondary schools.
>
> From conversations in the staffroom, you'd be forgiven for thinking that the parents were either about to parachute a crack team of Ofsted inspectors in or they were at the school gates with pitchforks and flaming torches. Parents were good for church services, school trips and sports days, very little else. School was the domain of the teachers and staff, and parents were to be kept in the playground. Ideally, the

two were not to meet. Despite the fact parents appeared to be, on the whole, supportive of the school and dominated the governing body, staff culture towards them was characterised by resentment and limited to meeting the statutory requirements, "Get 'em in and out as quick as possible".

It was only after moving to a school down the road, which viewed parents as collaborative partners, that I was able to see how limited my interactions with parents and carers were. My new setting did things very differently; teachers had a presence on the playground at the start and the end of the day. This allowed me to build relationships with parents from the very start of the school year, day-in day-out. I was able to speak with parents over the smallest of issues, to put their minds at ease and let them know I was there for them just as much as their child.

It was the norm that staff were present, seen out and about. Whilst teaching staff being present at the start and end of the school day is a minor thing, it epitomised the school's attitude to working and engaging with all parents. It allowed for an 'in' for those parents who couldn't make parents' evening, it meant that parents who didn't want to come into the building, for whatever reason, could still bring their concerns to the table, and it allowed issues to be nipped in the bud before they could grow into a thorn. Relationships started small and became more and more meaningful.

The ethos to working to parents was modelled by senior leadership; they went out of their way to set clear expectations on how to engage with parents. They led the way for all staff to see how it was done. Leadership would drop into meetings with parents and be part of the conversation; this made staff feel supported during those potentially 'tricky' conversations and helped parents know that all levels of staff cared about them and what they had to say.

I suppose what, I'm trying to say is that the differences between the two schools boiled down to cultures and attitude towards working with parents. By having a leadership team who set out clear expectations of working with all parents, encouraging teachers to actively engage with those parents who find working with the school allowed for those relationships to be built and the barriers to come down. Ultimately, this built trusting and open relationships between staff and those caring for the pupils we worked with. Staff didn't view engaging with parents as a chore, but as a central facet of their roles. Once trust was built, parents who were struggling were able to come to the school for support on a number of issues, ranging from domestic violence to putting food on the shelves, this had untold benefits for the pupils in our care.

Alex's Top Tips:

1 Don't use jargon.

Education is full of subject-specific language; we use it all the time without even thinking about it. Now, consider a parent who might not have a wide vocabulary or the language skills to express themselves clearly. Using language which they will not be familiar with will only serve to prevent clear dialogue and meaningful relationships.

2 Start Early
   Looking to build relationships with parents at the first parents' evening of the year is too late. Consider your new intake, or the pupils you will work with the following year. How can you get to know the pupils, their parents, and their needs?
3 Differentiate
   Just like we differentiate for the needs of pupils, we should differentiate for the needs of parents. You will encounter parents with an array of needs, and not all of them will need the same level of support. Making extra arrangements to meet or support parents may add to your workload, but in the long run it will support parental engagement with the child's educational journey.
4 Identify who the 'hard-to-reach' parents are
   Working with colleagues or using data to identify parents who you will want to target for relationship building will give you a better idea of where you will want to focus your efforts. Going into the year 'blind' as to who may require extra support may be too late.
5 Don't let reputations affect your relationship
   We all know *that* family who have been challenging or with whom colleagues may have had difficult conversations. One of the joys of a new academic year is that it offers an opportunity to have a fresh start. Be aware of what has happened in the past and the baggage parents come with, but your new year is your tabula rasa. Start from the ground up, not mid-argument.
6 Let them know you are human
   Of course, there are professional boundaries but letting people know your interests and hobbies helps parents to know that there is more to you than planning, teaching and marking. Through this, common ground and shared interests can be fostered, and this will help in building relationships.
7 Be honest about mistakes and successes
   Humans make mistakes. We all get things wrong from time to time. Part of leaning from them is being open and honest about it. Being able to share when things have gone well, or not so well, with parents will help to build trust it shows a willingness to reflect and improve. This will help you as a practitioner, identify areas of your practice you may wish to avoid and repeat.
8 Network
   You school or setting may not have all the answers to support all the needs of your parents, but you will know where to find them. Don't be afraid of ringing charities or external partners when looking to help parents and careers. This will put a wider array of tools, knowledge and skills at your disposal.
9 Don't take anything for granted
   Regardless of your pupil intake, you could be in a leafy suburb or in an inner-city school. No two families are the same, just as no two pupils are the same. Treat each case, each person as a unique situation. Sure, there it may be helpful to identify similarities, just as this may be misleading. By not making assumptions or presumptions, you will avoid faux pas and causing offence. If you are unsure of a situation or circumstance, or the right way of going about things, ask.

Barriers to parental engagement in education

Conducting a self-review on the current practice, celebrating successful parental engagement, whilst analysing potential barriers, establishes a clear ownership of change.

Bryk and Schneider (2002) discuss the lack of 'relational trust' between parents and teachers. By understanding this context further, the identification of methods and fresh clarity to overcome these challenges, presents itself almost as fresh data to analyse. Adams and Christenson (2000) identify trust as a key element to mutual respect and understanding; without this, relationships are already at a disadvantage. One example of how trust can be tarnished is due to the lack of time that teachers and parents get to talk or communicate with one another. This can come across negatively to parents, who feel that teachers may be 'out of touch' with their needs.

However, it is important to understand the complexity of this topic, as many areas overlap and can be far more difficult to distinguish. "Interpersonal communication is intentionally or unintentionally affecting others by transmitting and receiving messages" (Korkut, 2000).

The relationship between school staff and families is commonly highlighted as one of the poignant areas for collaborative success. However, many more areas ultimately impact this meaningful and fragile relationship. Gisewhite (2021) identified some of the key reasons as to why this may be the case, along with the recognition that some teachers come into the professional ill-equipped to deal with these relationships: "establishing teacher training for effective communication with parents and discuss how this lens, could address commonly encountered communication barriers".

Research into wider contributors that impact engagement includes:

- ICT Barriers
- Lack of sufficient staff/teacher training on how to effectively work with families
- Lack of variety and trust regarding volunteering opportunities for families
- Negative association with particular staff members, linked to own school experience/child's previous school.
- COVID – Physical and mental health impacted by the pandemic
- Separated families
- Engaging dads
- Multicultural families
- Attendance
- Domestic abuse
- Parental pride
- Challenging behaviour with other children – Often making their other children late for school.

The diagram below (Figure 5.1) highlights identified barriers to engagement within education. Feedback was generated through my own academic research, personal experiences and Twitter polls.

By understanding barriers and the importance of parents as co-educators, school mindsets and communication methods are challenged (Groves et al., 2008). Changing the narrative on how schools communicate and work with parents can impact on the relationships themselves. Hargreaves and Wall (2002) describe the context of 'formal' meetings and the stress and anxiety that can be felt during this time.

Engaging the disengaged and overcoming barriers 103

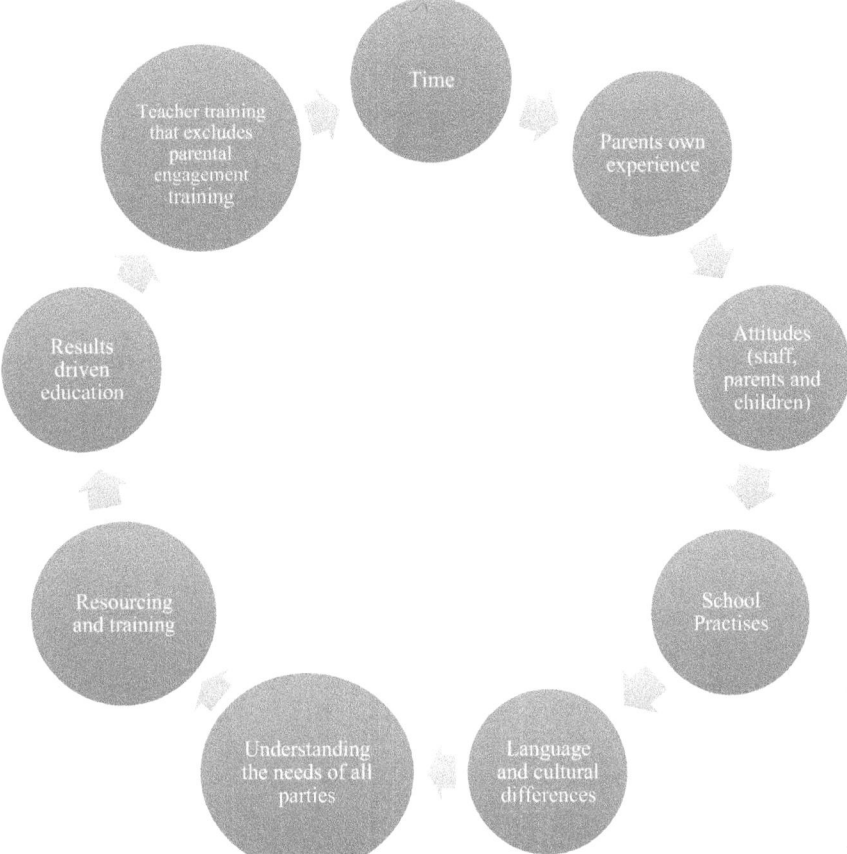

Figure 5.1 A circular flow chart consisting of nine circles that each hold an identified area linked to barriers to engagement within education. There are grey arrows in between each circle, all moving in a clockwise direction. Each circle holds a caption linked to a different barrier.

Dr Chris Martin reflects on what parental engagement means to him, reflecting on how the best education for children is deeply rooted by effective partnerships of parents and schools.

Dr Chris Martin, Honorary Research Fellow in Education, University of Wolverhampton

Much research has been conducted into parental engagement in children's education, with many studies arriving at similar conclusions (Sacker et al., 2002; Hornby & Lafaele, 2011; Hill et al., 2018); parents' engagement with their child's education fluctuates and is dependent on several factors such as socio-economic status, parental level of education and the age and ability of the child. As a child grows older and progresses through the education system, parental engagement weakens with a shift towards aspirations rather than academic outcomes. A further weakening factor suggested by Hornby and Lafaele (2011) could be the stability of the family unit, for example single-parent family status, ill health, or disability.

It is important to note that 'parental engagement' is challenging to define, as highlighted in previous studies (McNeal, 2001; Martin, 2020) and definitions tend to be based on the most salient features across the research literature. Epstein (1995) defined parental engagement as having six facets: parenting, communicating, volunteering, learning at home, decision-making and collaborating with the community. These were later reduced by McNeal (2001) to four: parent–child discussion, monitoring, involvement in school and classroom activities, and participation in school organisation. Finally, Johnson and Hull (2014) suggested that these could be further summarised into three categories: home-based involvement, school-based involvement, and parents' educational aspirations (p. 407).

It is incredibly difficult to separate parental engagement from Bourdieu's (1986) notions of 'capital' and 'habitus', both of which play pivotal roles in parental engagement in education. Ultimately, it is parents who transmit educational capital in the form of educational values and beliefs in children through their 'habitus', the environment within which children are raised. If parents do not place an importance on education and learning, then education professionals need to work twice as hard not only to encourage and engage children, but also to engage with parents. Parents who do attach importance could be more successful in forging effective relationships with their child's school and engage with their learning.

There is research to suggest (Bubić & Tošić, 2016; Martin, 2020) that some parents disengage with school activities due to a perceived power dynamic – teachers are seen as superior, and some parents feel inferior, or even embarrassed, to visit school through lack of confidence and possibly negative experiences of schooling. Some parents are uncomfortable with this dynamic (Crozier, 1999) and therefore disengage. Maintaining regular contact with parents on their child's successes and concerns could go some way to changing this perception. School ethos is important in terms of establishing a culture of maintaining close contact with parents. In independent schools, for example, there tends to be more contact with parents than in state schools, which has certainly been the case anecdotally.

There is strong evidence that indicates that parents get involved in their child's education to varying degrees and that the reasons for these fluctuations are multi-faceted. Educational establishments (schools, colleges, universities) have the responsibility of maintaining effective communication with parents regarding the education and wellbeing of their children. For some parents, this communication can be hampered by negative perceptions of these establishments due to adverse experiences in their own education and it is here where regular communication is key – regular communication with parents could go some way to breaking down these barriers through positive exposure to discussions of success and progress in their child's education, and, where deemed necessary, provide further support for parents who do not feel confident with helping their child with homework or other extended learning opportunities. This could be something as simple as suggesting that the child attends a breakfast club or a homework club after school, where school staff could be on hand to support with more academically challenging work and give the child access to learning resources which they may not have at home.

> Securing the best education for children is deeply rooted in the effective partnerships of parents and schools – there should be a reciprocal relationship between both parties with the sole interest of supporting the development and education of children. Schools and other educational establishments should have an awareness of the potential barriers to parental engagement and should work with parents at every given opportunity to overcome them.

Where do we go from here?

Every staff member has a significant role and, in terms of next steps, this will vary slightly depending both on the individual and on the context of the respective school. However, each one of these vital cogs needs to have the following: hope, trust, a sense of worth and the opportunity to evolve and grow. Once each of these areas have been nourished and provided with the necessary support to meet their needs, the ship then moves forward – full steam ahead! It is a carefully oiled machine that is nurtured, understood and continues to advance.

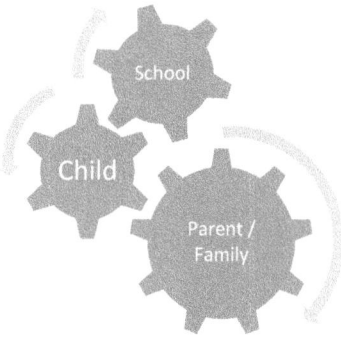

Figure 5.2 Three cogs interlinked with arrows around them symbolising their collaborative movement. Each cog has a different word/phrase inside of it.

We have discussed the significance of identifying and overcoming barriers to parental engagement, with recognition around the positive outcomes that can be achieved for the children. Family–school relationships can realign the boundaries within education as conditions change to enable successful collaborative. Stewart (2008) identified the importance of emotional engagement regarding academic performance.

It is undeniable that, as educators, we want the very best for our students, and they are often at the very forefront of our minds, in every decision we make and every plan we construct. But taking a moment to stop, to step back and to look at the people behind the child, could be one of the most important reflections to make. They are the audience we need to reach; they are the cog that we need to nurture continuously to ensure that it works in synchronicity with the child and school.

It is important not to presume, but to understand a family's dynamics. There will be visible objectives and elements that we, as educators, are very aware of and then there will be those that are less obvious.

Whilst many schools achieve great success with regards to welcoming families, a reflective approach to current practice is always encouraged– an engagement audit if you will!

Society is changing, family's needs are evolving, and schools must apply an innovative and diverse approach to identify a change in need. If a school maintains a similar pattern of engagement, the same families will be repeatedly missed. To change the approach is to change the outcome; by understanding each circumstance it provides us with the opportunity for a diversified approach within our school communities.

Successful engagement is not just about schools inviting families to events that they have planned and booked into the academic diary for the year ahead, or, in many cases, regurgitated year after year. Successful engagement is working in collaboration with families – working together, covering the daily functions and foundations of the school. This needs careful management and an understanding of how it may be slow to get the wheels in motion initially. However, the rewards for your time, compassion, shared approach and cumulative effort will result in a powerful force for good.

There will be visible and invisible elements to disengagement. One must not succeed the other, as both stand equally in the face of inclusion.

> **Inclusion:**
>
> 1. The action or state of being included within a group or structure.
> 2. The practice or policy of providing equal access to opportunities and resources for people who might otherwise be excluded or marginalized, such as those who have physical or intellectual disabilities and members of other minority groups.
>
> Oxford Languages Dictionary

Overcoming barriers

Recent ideology surrounding the important connection between families and school identifies possibilities for radical change: "Changing the way schools perceive appropriate and consistent parent involvement could assist in moving towards greater parent engagement" (Timberly et al., 2016).

In England, the 1997 White Paper, 'Excellence in Schools', provided a strategy for securing parental involvement. Within the paper, three key strategies were highlighted: Giving parents a voice; Providing parents with information; and Encouraging parental partnerships with schools. "Parents are a child's primary educator and our partnership approach will involve them fully. We want to put the years of division, conflict and short-term thinking behind us" (White Paper: Excellence in Schools, 1997, p. 12). Whilst the report concludes five different avenues for this to be executed, the guidance to deliver this is left to the discretion of individual educational establishments, leaving potential gaps for errors, inconsistency and unrealistic frameworks on how to achieve this.

With a clear approach and robust framework, it is undoubtedly the case that evidence concludes partnership working to be a successful approach for schools to improve outcomes. The government's strategy identified a wide range of activities, including: parent governor roles, the provision of prospectuses and annual reports, home–school agreements, involvement in inspection processes, and the provision of information about curriculum and school performances (Desforges and Abouchaar, 2003).

When guidance and strategies have been executed correctly, and with consideration to all involved, the results are unmistakable: "The evidence is now beyond dispute. When schools work together with families to support learning, children tend to succeed not just in school, but throughout life" (Henderson and Berla, 1994).

The ideology challenging a common approach in schools is around 'telling' parents information or agendas, rather than creating narratives collaboratively. This one-dimensional communication is often mistaken as 'jointly engaging parents in dialogue'. Raffaele and Knoff (1999) share the importance of home–school collaboration being built on a foundation of core beliefs and a proactive rather than reactive approach: "the engagement of all parents should be worked for". Moss, Petrie and Poland (1999) explain that the knowledge parents hold is vital to embracing the whole child, rather than disregarding their position. By changing this approach, the doors of communication open more freely, benefitting everyone involved. As a result of this dialogue, the vital levels of trust can be increased (Lopez, et al., 2001).

Caplan (2000) shared the notion that students attain more educational success when schools and families work together collaboratively and, as previously identified, there are multiple ways to do this, and activities can be split into short-, medium- and long-term plans. Some of the quicker ideas to implement include:

- Make positive phone calls home – from all members of staff.
- Begin to establish a Parent Council.
- Hold regular drop-in meetings at different times and in different locations.
- Have regular and meaningful parental meetings – listen to their voice.
- Share your vision with the whole-school community – What does your new way of working with families mean for staff/the pupils/families/governors/PTFA? Identify clear foundations for everyone.
- Maintain the narrative – Don't set high expectations and let them slip. People will only lose faith in future initiatives.
- Let parents know how important they are to you and your school.
- Send a certificate home to every parent twice a year – E.g. 'Thank you for consistently reading with your child', 'Thank you for instilling the importance of friendship in your child, they are a valuable member of Year 2 and school community'.

Parent councils – Bridging barriers

The ideology behind Parent Council groups is to develop relationships with both existing and new parents., This will help to bridge the communication gap, increasing partnership working and helping families to have a better understanding of how children are being taught in school (Caplan, 2000; Drake, 2000; Moorman, 2002).

Parent voluntary action groups can have a direct and powerful approach to instigate this long-term narrative: "role construction is also shaped by the expectations of individuals and groups important to the parent, about the parent's responsibilities relevant to the child's schooling" (Hoover-Dempsey et al., 2005). Such engagement can lead to increased learning opportunities that can stay with children throughout their education: "parental involvement has been positively linked to indicators of student achievement, including teacher ratings of student competence, student grades" (Deslandes et al., 1999).

Voluntary action groups can include a wide variety of engagement opportunities for parents. The Plowden Report (Plowden, 1967) emphasised the importance and value of parents being involved within the wider school community. There has been evidence to suggest that the sooner this starts in a child's life, the more impactful it can be to the child:

"parental engagement and involvement naturally changes as a child gets older, its greatest impact is on a child's early years" (Ellison-Lee and Coates, 2021). The importance and significant value of the early years form the basis of Epstein's (1986) notion that "the overlap between the three spheres of home, school and community provides a more supportive developmental environment for children". With this important triangular approach, the link between the early years and primary education remains of key significance to both the child and the family.

The importance of engagement with parents was highlighted within the government's core purpose document Foundation Years: Sure Start Children Centre's (2013b), which addresses the importance of engaging with parents. This includes the significance of parental voice, which is highlighted as a keynote within chapter 2 of the Sure Start children's centres statutory guidance (2013a) "take into account the views of local families and communities in deciding what is sufficient children's centre provision" (DfE, 2013a). With the drastic disappearance of many Sure Start Children's Centres, a huge gap has been left and this is strongly felt by communities: "the UK's flagship early years programme [has been] 'hollowed out' and [is] in decline" (Butler, 2018). The gap of supporting families, especially within the early stages of their children's lives, leaves a huge void for families and the early years/education system. If families do not engage with nursery/toddler groups, then school is likely to be their first formal port of communication. A survey conducted by 4Children in 2011 identified that 87% of Children Centres were using volunteers, highlighting a powerful strong link to the local community and a recognised willingness of families to work collaboratively. The important role of community action now falls significantly to schools, and the responsibility to collaborate with communities continues to intensify as additional resources diminish.

Given the increasing absence of Children Centres and the importance of community links, as directed by DfE reports, it is important to understand that for success to come to fruition, we must view families, not just the child: "If educators view children simply as students, they are likely to see the family as separate from the school" (Epstein, 1986). The government document, Foundation Years: Sure Start Children Centre's (2013), identified the importance of engaging with families as early as possible in a child's life, and this remains one of the most pivotal narratives available – plant the seeds early and watch them grow!

To understand the narrative from parent-supporting-schools to parental engagement in children's learning, Kim (2009) identified the differing relationships and responsibilities between the two. Recognising that schools and parents understand the importance of their roles, both individually and collaboratively, helps to develop the whole child through a collaborative approach. 'School, family and community partnership', as recognised and emphasised by Epstein and Sheldon's research (2007), who identified the shared responsibility of children's learning.

Time to open the doors

It is evident to see that voluntary action within schools is fast becoming normal practice, with fundraising for equipment and the generosity of donations (uniform, food, time) becoming common practice.

The co-production of a Parent Council will support this notion and needs to become part of the fundamental foundations of a school's core practice and values, to become the new common framework for engagement with families.

Welcoming parents into the school shows them that they are trusted, valued and appreciated. The development of my own Parent Council saw the significant impact of adopting this approach with the projects that we represented and the areas of development that we were keen to support within the school.

The sooner this is implemented, the better, as it can take time to build momentum, achieve groups' long-term goals and gather evidence for inspections.

St Nicholas Parent Council's Key Achievements and Projects:

- Attending school dinners with the children; structure of lunchtime, sampling the food that was offered to the children, speaking to the staff on duty, running logistics, potential areas to improve, pupil voice and staff voice.
- Working in partnership with other schools to help them develop their own council; Opportunity to share best practice and work collaboratively to strengthen outcomes and opportunities.
- Setting up an emergency breakfast scheme to feed children that come into school hungry in the morning; Completed in collaboration with a food bank charity. Council members had asked for information on whether children come to school equipped and able to learn effectively. This raised the topic of children not having breakfast before school. Whilst the school did already support these children, it became evident that a sufficient supply of long-life food would be beneficial for the children and provide a well-stocked supply of food for staff to access when needed.
- Assisting with school policies – Behaviour and Homework; Policies were read, reflected upon and parent voice was filtered back to the group with suggested amendments.
- Assisting with the school's Statutory Inspection of Anglican Methodist Schools (SIAMS) visit
- Partnership working with charities – The Rainbow Centre
- Collaborating with teaching and leadership staff; Subject leads would run through the structure of a lesson and explain how the scheme of work supports children's development and understanding from Reception to Year 6. Homework was also explained and demonstrated as to how it supports the learning in school.
- Assisting with the development of the school's new PoPA group (formally PTFA)
- The Council's success was shared and presented at Sheffield's Voluntary Sector Studies Network and Canterbury Christ Church University
- Working with the head of maths to develop a 'working with parents' maths scheme.
- Published within; 'The Four Pillars of Parental Engagement' (Robbins and Dempster, 2021), 'The Mentally Healthy Schools Workbook' (Knightsmith, 2020), *Primary Times Magazine*, VSR Publications 'Parent Councils and Partnership Working in Schools (2019) and Parentkind UK 'Successful School Parent Council' (2018)

Through times of adversity, we have proven that even in the most challenging of situations, there are very dedicated parents who are willing to collaborate. They just need the opportunity to be presented to them.

However, as much as this concept may make some schools feel nervous, the proof of its success is clear to see. By working together and focussing on the issues most important to the families within the community, the Parent Council was able to support the improvement of learning outcomes, parental engagement, and the communication between teachers and leadership staff and the wider community.

Parents should be viewed as an extremely positive source of voluntary support. The generosity, and the skill set available, should be utilised as much as possible. Getting to know the parents, their interests, jobs, skills, talents, interests and hobbies, provides schools with a full and enriched skill base to work with. Our council members included designers, crafts people, salespeople and administrators. As a result, we had professional branding and status within the school, a successful and proactive council and new PoPA team– not bad for a school within a deprived area and no previous experience of having a Parent Council.

One thing has become evident to see: that a group of committed parents can make such a difference to their children's education and school experience. By welcoming a team of parents into your school and ensuring a whole-school approach – results can be achieved, in many shapes and forms.

References

Adams, K.S. and Christenson, S.L. (2000). Trust and the Family-School Relationship Examination of Parent-Teacher Differences in Elementary and Secondary Grades. Accessed 26th October 2021. https://www.sciencedirect.com/science/article/pii/S0022440500000480

Bourdieu, P. (1986) The forms of capital. in Richardson, J. G.(ed). *Handbook of Theory and Research for the Sociology of Education.* New York: Greenwood Press.

Bryk, A.S. and Schneider, B.L. (2002). *Trust in Schools: A Core Resource for Improvement.* New York: Russell Sage Foundation Publications.

Bubić, A. and Tošić, A. (2016). The relevance of parents' beliefs for their involvement in children's school life. *Educational Studies*, 42(5), pp. 519–533.

Butler, P. (2018). The Guardian: 1,000 Sure Start Children's Centre may have shut since 2010. Accessed 19th January 2022. https://www.theguardian.com/society/2018/apr/05/1000-sure-start-childrens-centres-may-have-shut-since-2010

Caplan, J.G. (2000). *Building Strong Family-School Partnerships to Support High Student Achievement.* The Informed Educator Series. Arlington, VA: Educational Research Service.

Crozier, G. (1999) Is it a case of 'We know when we're not wanted'? The parents' perspective on parent-teacher roles and relationships. *Educational Research*, 41(3), pp. 315–328.

Desforges, C. and Abouchaar, A. (2003) *The impact of parental involvement, parental support and family education on pupil achievement and adjustment: A literature review.* London: Department for Education and Skills

Deslandes, R., Royer, E., Potvin, P. and Leclerc, D. (1999). Patterns of home and school partnership for general and special education students at the secondary level. *Exceptional Children*, 65(4), pp. 496–506.

DfE. (2013a). Sure Start Children's Centre's statutory guidance. Accessed 2nd June 2023. https://assets.publishing.service.gov.uk/government/uploads/system/uploads/attachment_data/file/678913/childrens_centre_stat_guidance_april-2013.pdf

DfE. (2013b). Foundation Years: Sure Start Children's Centre's. Accessed 18th January 2022. https://publications.parliament.uk/pa/cm201314/cmselect/cmeduc/364/36407.htm#note182

Drake, D.D. (2000). Parents and families as partners in the education process: Collaboration for the success of students in public schools. *ERS Spectrum*, 18(2), pp. 34–39.

Education Endowment Foundation. (2021a). Parental Engagement. Moderate impact for very low cost based on extensive evidence. Accessed 24th February 2021. https://educationendowmentfoundation.org.uk/education-evidence/teaching-learning-toolkit/parental-engagement

Education Endowment Foundation. (2021b). Working with parents to support children's learning. Accessed 10th January 2022. https://educationendowmentfoundation.org.uk/education-evidence/guidance-reports/supporting-parents

Ellison-Lee, D. and Coates, D.S. (2021). Effective parental engagement: A handbook for schools. Accessed 17th January 2022. https://unitedlearning.org.uk/Portals/0/Parental%20Engagement%20Handbook%20-%20United%20Learning%20%28v3%29_1.pdf

Epstein, J.L. (1986). Parent's reactions to teacher practises of parental involvement. *The Elementary School Journal*, 86(3), pp. 277–294.

Epstein, J.L. (1995). School/family/community partnerships: Caring for the children we share. *The Phi Delta Kappa*, 76(9), pp. 701–712.

Epstein, J.L. and Sheldon, S.B. (2007). Improving student attendance with school, family and community partnerships. *The Journal of Educational Research*, 100(5), pp. 267–275. http://www.jstor.org/stable/27548191

Gisewhite, R. (2021). A call for ecologically based teacher-parent communication skills training in pre-service teacher education programmes. Accesses 20th October 2021. https://www.tandfonline.com/doi/abs/10.1080/00131911.2019.1666794

Goodall, J. (2012). Parental engagement to support children's learning: A six point model. *School Leadership and Management*, 33, 2. DOI:10.1080/13632434.2012.724668

Groves, M., Baumber, J. et al (2008). Regenerating SCHOOLS: Leading the transformation of standards and services through community engagement. Continuum International Publishing Group Network Continuum

Hargreaves, K. and Wall, D. (2002). 'Getting Used to Each Other': Cross-phases liaison and induction. In *Transfer in the Classroom: 20 Years On*, edited by L. Hargreaves and M. Galton, 28–53. London: Routledge Falmer.

Harris, A. and Goodall, J. (2007). Engaging Parents in Raising Achievement: Do Parents Know They Matter? Research Report DCSF-RW004. University of Warwick. Department for Children, Schools and Families.

Henderson, A.T. and Berla, N. (1994). *A New Generation of Evidence: The Family is Critical to Student Achievement*. Washington, DC: National Committee for Citizens in Education.

Hill, N.E., Witherspoon, D.P. and Bartz, D. (2018). Parental involvement in education during middle school: Perspectives of ethnically diverse parents, teachers, and students. *The Journal of Educational Research*, 111(1), pp. 12–16.

Hoover-Dempsey, K.V. (2005). Why do parents become involved? Accessed 3rd March 2021. http://www.jstor.org/stable/10.1086/499194

Hornby, G. and Lafaele, R. (2011). Barriers to parental involvement in education: An explanatory model. *Educational Review*, 63(1), pp. 37–52.

Johnson, U.Y. and Hull, D.M. (2014). Parental involvement and science achievement: A cross-classified multilevel latent growth curve analysis. *The Journal of Educational Research*, 107(5), pp. 339–409.

Kim, Y. (2009). Minority parental involvement and school barriers: Moving the focus away from deficiencies of parents. *Educational Research Review*, 4(2), pp. 80–102.

Knightsmith, P. (2020). *The mentally healthy schools workbook*. London: Jessica Kingsley Publishers.

Korkut, F. (2000). Effective communication skills, types of conflict solving and teamwork, seminar notes of educator and supervisor. Ankara Egitim-Sen Publications.

Lopez, G.R., Scribner, J.D. and Mahitivanichcha, K. (2001). Redefining parental involvement: Lessons from high-performing migrant-impacted schools. *American Educational Research Journal*, 38(2), pp. 253–288.

Martin, C. (2020). Response to 'The motivational dimension of language teaching' (Lamb, 2017). *Language Teaching*, 52(3), pp. 233–236.

McNeal, R.B. (2001) Differential effects of parental involvement on cognitive and behavioural outcomes by socioeconomic status. *Journal of Socioeconomics*, 30(2), pp. 171–179.

Moorman, J. (2002). Using the McDonald's approach to generate parent involvement. *Principal*, 81(5), pp. 48–49.

Moss, P., Petrie, P. and Poland, G. (1999). *Rethinking School: Some International Perspectives*. London: National Youth Agency.

Oxford Languages Dictionary. (2023). Accessed 24th March 2021. https://languages.oup.com/google-dictionary-en/

Parczewska, T. (2020). Difficult situations and ways of coping with them in experiences of parent's home schooling their children during the COVID-19 pandemic in Poland. Accessed 14th March 2021 https://doi.org/10.1080/03004279.2020.1812689

Plowden Report. (1967). Children and their Primary Schools: A report of the Central Advisory Council for Education (England).

Raffaele, L.M. and Knoff, H.M. (1999). Improving home-school collaboration with disadvantaged families: Organizational principles, perspectives, and approaches. *School Psychology Review*, 28(3), pp. 448–466.

Robbins, J. and Dempster, K. (2021). *The Four Pillars of Parental Engagement*. Wales: Independent Thinking Press.

Sacker, A., Schoon, I. and Bartley, M. (2002). Social inequality in educational achievement and psychosocial adjustment throughout childhood: Magnitude and mechanisms. *Social Science & Medicine*, 55(5), pp. 863–880.

Stewart, E.B. (2008). School structural characteristics, student effort, peer associations, and parental involvement: The influence of school – and individual-level factors on academic achievement. *Education and Urban Society*, 40, pp. 179–204.

Timberly, L., Baker, J.W., Gwendolyn, K. and Russel, J.S. (2016). Identifying barriers: Creating solutions to improve family engagement. Accessed 22nd October 2021. https://files.eric.ed.gov/fulltext/EJ1124003.pdf

White Paper: Excellence in Schools. (1997). Excellence in schools. Accessed 27th July 2022. http://www.educationengland.org.uk/documents/wp1997/excellence-in-schools.html

6 Parental engagement
A comparison between mainstream and SEN schools

Catherine McClenaghan

I have been working in the field of education for more than eleven years and have had the chance to experience it from different angles; the TA, the 1:1, the teacher, the in-home behavior support, and the parent workshop facilitator. I've also had the chance to work in the field in different settings; mainstream, SEN and the home. Finally, I have had the chance to work across the North of Ireland, England, Boston, Australia and Abu Dhabi. Many factors changed throughout the years, but the constant was that I remained within the field of education with my passion and focus being Special educational needs and disability (SEND). I studied Applied Behavior Analysis and was so fortunate for all the opportunities that the master's course allowed. I studied and became a Board-Certified Behavior Analyst (BCBA) working in the home with parents and families and in other school settings.

When I tell people that I am a BCBA, I'm usually met with one of two reactions: a curious 'Oh wow, very good' or a disapproving curt reply. While I've come across many individuals with discomfort or disdain for the background I studied (Behavior Analysis) most have said that this is due to them having heard about certain practices that have been used in the past. I will be the first to agree that there have been many practices used in the field many years ago which I don't condone and would never think of using. However, I will point out, that every field has bad practitioners, and those individuals shouldn't set the tone for everyone in the field, or the field itself.

Teaching in mainstream education was initially something that I had a niggling worry about as I wasn't sure how inclusion would truly work to ensure every child receives an excellent education. Warnock's (1978) initial report largely drove the push for inclusive education for those with Special Educational Needs (SEN) in mainstream schools, yet the author later questioned this wave and wasn't sure if it was working (2005). Having worked as a TA and a 1:1 in mainstream and SEN settings, I often wondered if children with Individual education plans (IEPs) or Educational, Health and Care Plans (EHCPs), despite people's good intentions, were set up to fail in the mainstream classroom. From my observations over the years in mainstream settings I noted time, training, burnout, and resources all play an important factor in the efficacy of inclusion.

On my journey to become a teacher I also experienced the mindset of an individual who challenged me as I was trying to ensure that those children with SEN in my class were catered for. I was making the point that there are more and more children with different needs in mainstream education and some strategies I had used previously; Picture exchange communication system (PECs), token economy, visual timetables, visual prompts, have proved to be effective when implemented in an individualised way for teaching certain skills. I was told that anything I do for the children with EHCPs (and those seeking this route) should not be at the expense of other children. I was told by that individual that 'those SEN children were the minority', and I am 'making provision for them to be included in the education system' but my 'focus should be on the rest of the class'. I was told 'to be mindful of their special educational needs but not at the expense of the rest of the class'.

I wholeheartedly disagreed with the viewpoints and immediately reported this individual and had no further conversations with them. What was even more frustrating was that the conversation arose as I was explaining why I wanted to use picture icons when introducing cue cards to teach children to solve episodes of conflict that arise during playtimes and in the classrooms. I couldn't comprehend how additional prompts and learning resources around the classroom and in my practice could harm anyone in the class. Had I have been younger and more impressionable with no prior experience to know that this person was, in my eyes, wrong, would I have adopted this mindset and then gone about my journey as a teacher? I dread to think but can confirm I don't see children with SEN as 'the minority' in the tone implied, nor do I feel they deserve any less focus than their peers. They perhaps might require us to use a different focus and look at different ways of teaching skills and facilitating learning, but they shouldn't have less of my attention. My passion and love for the field of education always brings me back to SEN and facilitating skill acquisition that makes a difference to the child and family.

I haven't yet been on the other side of the playground as a parent. In a teaching post I did notice that unless a child has had something out of the ordinary occur during the day, I could go from Monday to Friday with nothing more than a wave and a nod from myself at the door. The parents waited a short distance away, close enough that they can see a signal that I may need to talk to them, but still far enough away that their child can feel as though they have had some space to promote independence.

On the occasion I had to pass a message to the parent, and I signaled that I'd like to talk to them, I could see the worry creep across their face. I could almost hear their thought: "Oh God, what have they done?" I also worried about calling them over as I sensed their dread of being called over in front of other parents. Working in mainstream was the first time I had ever encountered this, although every teacher and parent with a child in mainstream said they were very familiar with 'the dread' or 'the wave'.

I was used to the parents being in the room with me, working alongside me and seeing in real time or first-hand what had happened in a session. In addition, I was used to going on a home visit once a week or having monthly meetings to discuss their progress. To combat this awkward exchange from both sides I would often signal a parent whilst shouting "Don't worry, everything is fine!", having instructed the child to celebrate on their way out and ensure that there were good messages that came after the dreaded signal!

Parental engagement

The research supports the view that the involvement of the parents and a collaborative relationship ultimately serves the child and boosts academic success and achievement along with higher rates of motivation (Rattenborg et al., 2018). This is great, considering that a recent survey across England, Wales and Northern Ireland reported that 85% of the parents who contributed to the Parents Voice Report in 2021 said they wanted to take a more active role in their child's education (Parentkind, 2021).

From a SEN perspective, however, this requires more thought when we as staff members approach and engage with the parents with the aim of getting them involved and working in a collaborative manner, as we are not privy to home life and the additional needs of the child and family.

When I carried out an initial literature search focusing on SEN, I was disheartened to find it return such little hits as most articles focused on mainstream education. This view was echoed by research carried out by Spear et al. (2021), who also noted a difference in the amount of literature focusing on parental engagement in SEN settings and for those with any SEND in a mainstream setting.

Research has suggested that students identified as having SEN are more at risk of poor educational and employment outcomes in comparison to those without (Prince et al., 2017). For many of those students with SEN, their success at school is largely influenced on their parents being actively involved and advocating for their needs and being familiar with the systems and language used (MacCormack et al., 2022). Some have argued that this collaboration between home and school is essential particularly for those with SEN (Scorgie and Sobsey, 2017).

What is parental engagement?

It might be easier to start off with what Parental Engagement is *not*. It is not persuading the parents to join in and comply with homework, nor is it simply showing up to the school for parents' evenings (Robbins and Dempster, 2021). Many publications seem to argue for different reasons why they prefer either the term 'involvement' or 'engagement', with some stating that the latter seems to be a better fit. There is always an underlying agreement about the crucial element of cooperation and collaboration between the family and the school.

While the semantics may play some importance in how messages are conveyed to the parents and the impact this has, my own personal view is that it doesn't really matter what we call it, engagement or involvement, the point is we, the village, are trying to get the child from where they are to where they need to be. The goal is the child achieving their best; in order to get there, we must work collaboratively.

When the COVID-19 pandemic first struck, school closures affected everyone, but for those in SEN settings this added an additional layer of complications, as the students also lost access to some very needed therapeutic services which they usually receive at school (O'Connor et al., 2021). Sadly, some research has suggested that many of those with SEND are more at risk of falling behind and staying behind (MacCormack et al., 2022). The schools ultimately had to rely on the parent to become the educator and the parent facilitated the online learning. Without this collaborative relationship, lessons could not have continued, and the child may have fallen behind as a result.

What is parental engagement to the parent?

I was curious to know what this term meant to the parents and so I reached out to ask a few. Where some parents replied or gave more information that was expanded upon, they have been given a number so show that it is the same parent's voice and view. While many gave different answers and viewpoints, there were similar themes that emerged from the responses.

Being involved

Many very simply felt it meant being actively involved in their child's education with the majority seeming to agree that it is their regular *involvement* with the school in order to support the child in their learning. Many echoed my own personal view, that it is all about the relationship between the school and home.

> Parental engagement to me is regular involvement with the school (key worker) around what the child needs and how they are doing. It can't be tokenistic and needs to be every term. I think parental engagement is or should be about us giving the school feedback on how the child is doing, what they are telling you, things that are going well, things that you have concerns about.
>
> Parent of SEND child in a mainstream setting

I think this is an extremely important point made by the parent, that engagement should involve parents giving their feedback on what is going well and what concerns a parent may have. It's not easy when a parent has a concern about something going on at school or something you are doing that they aren't sure about. However, if they know they can approach the school and discuss it, this makes everything easier. This parent values being able to give the school feedback, which ultimately serves the school. Whether this is something going well or something that needs to be discussed, then having that feedback is great. One recent survey of parents showed that only 54% said the school implemented suggestions from feedback, with only 51% reporting that they felt they had a say (ParentKind, 2021).

When placed in a mainstream setting, I taught a child with SEN. We had noticed at school that they didn't have a reliable way of communicating, and their repertoire was quite limited. They didn't communicate any basic wants or needs. One Monday, the parent mentioned to the child's 1:1 that the weekend had been particularly tough in terms of challenging behaviour. We invited the parent to come for a chat after school on a day that suited them. This was the type of conversation I loved. As I had previously been in the home setting working so closely with parents on a 1:1 basis with their child, I felt so comfortable. The parent was able to discuss challenges at home, we problem solved and came up with some targets to work on.

In the meantime, I had offered some suggestions that I had put in place in class and which might work at home. This child didn't seem to be able to request attention from staff or peers in a socially appropriate way; instead, they seemed to resort to pushing peers, destroying property etc. We had been working on having them request this attention by tapping an adult and saying "Excuse me", which the adult would praise this method of gaining attention. We ignored or didn't make a fuss of previously used but inappropriate guaranteed ways of gaining attention and noticed that the rates of inappropriate behaviour decreased significantly. We then expanded this target by teaching them to go and seek the adult or peer from other places in the room. They learned so quickly and we saw this skill allow them to independently request the attention of any adult in the room from any distance.

I modelled what this looked like, along with a few other communication skills and targets with the child as the parent watched with the 1:1. When the adults were engaged in conversation, the child set down their book, tapped my shoulder with "Excuse me" to which I replied "Thank you for saying excuse me, what's up?" I was so pleased and proud when they said, "I want go home." We squealed with delight as this was a completely novel and independent request, and so appropriate having been at school for an additional 45 minutes!

Afterwards, the 1:1 told me that the parent had cried when I left, as they didn't know their child was able to do most of what they had seen that afternoon, joking that they'd like to take me home with them. That really hit home for me how important their feedback is in this setting, and for them to be actively involved in the process. This regular follow-up about what was working well meant I could always be using my BCBA hat to think outside the box in terms of individualized strategies to support the family by teaching and implementing targets at school that the family could use at home.

Not all feedback is going to be positive; some can be a bit more awkward. When working in the UAE there were a lot of cultural factors that, as a person from a different country and religion, I had to be aware of. I worked in a SEN school for children with high support needs. One child on my caseload found communication to be challenging and would often engage in aggressive and self-injurious behaviour if denied access to something. Towards the end of my year working with this child, on a routine weekly home visit their parent disclosed that the child had begun to masturbate in public rooms in the house. There were many guests that came to the house and so this had become a problem. The parent seemed quite uncomfortable initially to broach the topic; however, I didn't really bat an eyelid or find the conversation in any way awkward. I had worked with many young males with similar support needs in residential settings where this situation had occurred, and they were engaging in this behaviour in public spaces. They learned to communicate vocally or use their Augmentative and alternative communication device (AAC) to request that they could go to their room and safely engage in this behaviour instead of in the classroom, the middle of a cafeteria or front lobby.

The parent disclosed that this was a concern for them as this behaviour isn't allowed in their religion and, in fact, they didn't want it to happen at all. I immediately felt completely out of my depth as the parent's concern was not which I shared and I immediately thought of how frustrating this would be for this young male if we were to completely deny access. I also wondered how we would even go about that. We had other parents at the school who felt differently and when similar situations arose they agreed that they wanted their child, who they thought 'Is going to do it anyway!', learn to communicate that they are leaving a room and that they go to a private area such as their bedroom.

While this parent was pleased with the other targets on their child's IEP, this was one area of concern that we had to respect their wishes and tread very carefully to ensure we consistently communicated with respect and understanding. The relationship never broke down and we continued to work in a collaborative manner for the short remaining weeks I was working with this child.

Communication

Parents seemed to agree about the communication from the school being an important factor in that they are aware of everything they need to be.

> I feel that it's all about how the school report to me and my husband and communicate the things we need to know.
>
> Parent of SEND child in a SEND setting

> I think it's about how the staff approach me and let me know what is going on and what my child has done or is learning. It's nice to have a short message if there was an issue so that if the child comes home upset I feel like I already know what the situation is. I do worry when I see the school's number come up on my phone when it isn't an emergency. I like Seesaw and Dojo as they were used during lockdown and have changed the way we all communicate. It's easier to engage with learning this way.
>
> Parent of SEND child in a SEND setting

What is parental engagement to staff?

My experience of talking to professionals within education found that most staff felt engagement is the parents being involved with the school and the child's education and learning. The idea of being involved is a similar and shared view held by both parties to be of importance in the process.

Involvement

> This is when parents play a full and active role in their child's education.
>
> Professional in education

While there is obviously more to this statement, it's a very simple start. For many parents and professionals, it might seem like an obvious statement, however, my own experience has taught me that some parents ultimately disagree with the idea that they need to be involved in their child's learning. There are many families who I have worked with who have felt that playing a role in their child's education is not their duty. In one mainstream setting I had a parent repeatedly tell me that educating their child was solely my job as their teacher. They didn't agree with homework or any further learning activities after school as they believed learning was supposed to take place at school.

Sadly, this child was so profoundly behind their peers and working outside of their year group and will likely remain this way throughout their educational journey without further opportunities to practice skills such as reading and writing. It was extremely upsetting at the time because the relationship between myself and the parents wasn't poor. We communicated every day at drop off and pick up. We would speak at length after school at pick up, and I would explain certain targets we were working on.

I asked if there could be some practice of counting items in the home and briefly explained the importance for the child to practice 1:1 correspondence. I asked if this is something they felt they could do and was met with such enthusiasm; however, when it came to discussing this as a follow-up I was then told that learning is supposed to happen at school, their child was to be taught by me, and it was not expected to continue at home. I feel that this was an example where there was a very clear misconception about our respective roles.

Communication

Most professionals seemed to believe that the fundamental element in parental engagement is communication.

> Put simply, engagement is crucial. There are many elements to it, but I feel communication is the crux.
>
> School staff and parents need to be able to work together and communicate effectively in all settings. When the relationship breaks down the impact is evident, I have learnt this the hard way as both a teacher and a parent.
>
> Previous Teacher in both Mainstream and SEN settings, SENDCo

In relation to communication, many agreed how important this element is to enable parental engagement, but that it shouldn't just come in the form of a notification or announcement.

> Parental engagement is a dialogue. It shouldn't just be emails/messages pushed out. You need to hear from your parent to understand the wider context.
>
> Previous Teacher #1 in both Mainstream and SEN settings, BESD school, SEN Further Education

> Parental engagement can take many forms but is essentially when parents take an active interest in their child's education and communicate effectively with the school. From a school's perspective it is about how they communicate effectively and clearly with parents so that they feel they are a valued partner and stakeholder in their child's schooling.
>
> Lead of specialist provision for students with profound, severe and complex learning needs

Parental engagement between the two settings

While many parents and staff offered their idea of what parental engagement is, there were some parents and staff who could offer an idea of how it differs between mainstream and SEN settings. While many of their opinions were similar in that engagement was, for them, the same across settings, some touched on the differences noted across settings.

Several parents reported that they felt their child's SEN setting was easier to engage with than a sibling's mainstream setting.

> My son is at a Special Needs School and I think they include me more than my daughter's school. I know what he is learning this week and this term and I am given ideas on how to extend that at home. There are many opportunities to talk to the teachers and staff in the morning as there are less children and the TAs are so great and watch the class if you need to talk. My daughter is at a mainstream school and I could go for weeks without knowing a thing. I also don't get any information out of her as she's at an age where she tells me she learned 'nothing' and did 'nothing' so I think this age (10 years old) is even more important for school to let parents know what is happening. The teachers always look so busy that unless you wait behind for such a long time until all children are picked up, you can't catch them. I will say that often I think 'No news is good news' as I'm sure I would be the first to know if she was misbehaving or falling behind.
>
> Parent of children in both Mainstream/SEN settings

This parent mentioned a few reasons why the SEN setting seems to be better, in her view, at engaging her with her son's education in comparison to her daughter's mainstream school. She acknowledged the fact that teachers had smaller class sizes in the SEN setting. She also mentioned the TAs taking the class in order for parents to have a quick chat in the mornings or afternoons. While this is great, it isn't always an option in any setting as some may have children with higher support needs and so often being a staff member down, even for a short period of time, can upset routines and lessons and can have a real impact on the running of the day. Having a key staff member who knows their child and any relevant situations would be most appropriate in larger classes to ensure someone can fit in a conversation around times that suit the parent.

As a staff member, I feel like one of the most important points in this reflection is what information this particular parent is interested in; what is going on in my child's day? When working in SEN settings I noted that parents wanted to know more about how their child was doing socially and emotionally, and to be kept in the loop about their therapies etc.

> My child has Cerebral Palsy. When the school check in weekly I'd rather know how my child feels at school and if they are integrating with friends. He also gets physio, so we like to know how that's going. I'm not as concerned about his grades just yet, so I like feedback about what I think is relevant now.
>
> Parent of child in SEN setting

Parents of a child with SEN in a mainstream setting seemed to mirror this view and wanted more information about their child's social development.

> I find it easier to just ask parents at the start of a term or year: what is your preferred method of contact and what information would you like to know regularly? Some parents are all about their child's academic attainment and others just want to know

> their child is happy and fitting in to their setting, whether that be mainstream or SEN. Knowing what each parent wants makes it easier to send out information and to address any concerns as they happen.
>
> Teacher in SEN setting, previously in mainstream

If parents are provided relevant information in advance, in a quick and time-efficient manner, then this gives them time to address any misconceptions, request additional information etc. I do feel the need to point out that not all parents want this information and hours of work teachers can spend making and sign posting parents to relevant material isn't always appreciated, and is even ignored by many. From a parent's perspective, they may not always have the time to sift through the material, and some aren't sure what is necessary and what is additional material.

> My daughter went from a mainstream primary school to a Special Needs Secondary school, while my son is undergoing the process of an Autism diagnosis. I haven't really noticed a difference between the two schools and how they approach me. I do feel that my daughters school used to contact me and give me more information in her first months as she was struggling initially and was requiring a lot more staff input. Now that she is settled, I hear from them less. I don't mind this though as I can see all the positive changes in her and I know that is down to the school.
>
> Parent #2 of children in both Mainstream and SEN settings

Like myself, there have been many who have worked in education and have been frustrated by the way in which the mainstream model of education is set up, particularly in relation to inclusion. I think that SEN schools have more experienced staff who are trained to work with children with higher support needs and are better equipped as schools, structurally, to support the needs of the children. There are usually higher staff ratios which significantly improve the level of support that can be offered.

> We have two children with SEN and EHCPs. One goes to an SEN school and the other is in mainstream and has a 1:1 there. The SEN school has so many more activities that we know help learning, but these aren't offered to our son in his mainstream school. His 1:1 is nice but I don't think she knows enough about his condition to support him. His teacher doesn't seem to know him. His EHCP targets are always really low and don't challenge him and at our daughter's school they are really pushing her. He has friends at school so we are reluctant to move him but I don't know if mainstream was the best decision.
>
> Parent of children in both Mainstream and SEN settings

A number of staff reported that they found the engagement process and relationship to occur more naturally when they worked in SEN settings than was the case in mainstream schools. This teacher acknowledges that not all SEN schools approach engagement correctly, but that they are more used to working as a team and collaborating to support the child.

> I feel special school settings have the head-start over mainstream for parental engagement, but this doesn't mean they always get it right. Special school staff are much more used to the team approach to supporting the child. Personally, I feel mainstream staff are often more defensive and worry about what is expected of them when actually they are looking for specialist guidance and advice too.
>
> Previous teacher in both Mainstream and SEN settings, SENDCo

In my experience, in SEND settings such as an SEN school, there naturally had to be more of a discussion between staff and families due to the nature of information that often had to be shared. Some young people attending an SEN school would have medical needs that staff had to be aware of, especially any significant changes. This meant more time given to the staff members before school was due to officially start. A lot of the settings I worked in, in many capacities, the settings had a more relaxed morning where the pace was more forgiving.

Barriers to successful engagement

My experience is limited to wearing the 'staff hat' and viewing engagement through this lens. There are so many factors and hurdles facing *all* parents when it comes to engaging with the school, but there were so many added layers of complexities when the child had any additional needs, and this isn't always understood by staff. Parents can often face additional challenges in social, psychological, and financial aspects (DePape and Lindsay, 2014).

Some parents choose not to tell anyone what additional barriers they face and so staff members may be unaware of what factors may hinder successful engagement and collaboration. Research suggests that parents of children with additional or complex needs can sometimes find engagement with the school more challenging (Lendrum, Barlow and Humphrey, 2013) and can have a host of other factors to contend with that makes engagement more complex, such as work/family conflicts (Stefanidis, King-Sears and Kyriakidou, 2021). Navigating the processes involved by the parents and the school requires a high level of consideration due to the complexities within both health and educational needs (Jigyel et al., 2019) and perhaps more light needs to be shed on the added barriers these parents face.

With a focus on SEN, I asked staff and parents what they feel are the biggest barriers to successful engagement. Their most common elements that emerged related to money, time, breakdowns in relationships and training.

Money

For all school leaders who are providing support and education for those SEN students, a lack of funding has proved to cause difficulty when it comes to support (Lamb, 2019). One report carried out by NAHT suggested that 73% of mainstream schools were especially struggling due to a decrease in funding, leading to TA cuts and staff shortages (BASW, 2018). I was implementing a typing target for a child with SEN in my classroom who had poor muscle tone and who, due to their needs, was unable to hold a pencil or control it enough to write legibly. At the time we had no budget to order a £29 keyboard that was tailored for SEN. We would have been able to afford it in a few months or the next term, but I didn't want to waste time, so I bought it myself. Had this child been in an SEN setting, the budget would have allowed many more resources.

Time

Lack of money can lead to staff shortages. I know myself that when my TA wasn't in, my exchanges with parents had to be brief as I was the only one able to oversee children coming in. This restricted the time I could afford parents of those children with SEN during contact hours. I know many ECTs who, in their training years, never had a TA for periods of weeks or months. Due to the increased workload and the stress involved in their planning, they said this directly affected the amount of time they felt they could chat with parents at pick-up/drop-off times or to arrange meetings outside contact hours.

In my class, a child had a 1:1 and this problem was able to be avoided as there was always, thankfully, that protected time for a parent and 1:1 support to have those conversations that were needed at pick up/drop off at the least. But what about the others in my class with additional needs that didn't yet have an EHCP to fund a 1:1? How could staff pass on messages to parents in these instances? The Family Liaison Officer (FLO) wasn't always free to fit in time for these messages. Also, as a teacher, particularly in a Key Stage 1 classroom without a TA, it would be nothing short of a miracle to get to the bathroom, let alone get out to pass on a message to the FLO for them to pass on to the parent.

I always felt as though I had a better relationship with parents, and saw a change in their child's learning, when I was able to frequently engage in a face-to-face manner. Even in as short as the 10-minute slots we had for parent teacher meetings. One term, many of the parents seemed to be thrown with the new content in mathematics and so I spent a lot of time showing some parents how to use the Part-Part Whole diagram to support their child at home. This was a really nice way to have that informal chat face to face rather than via a screen or written (formal) communication. It was useful to allow them to discuss areas of concern at home to ask them where they felt they needed most support. Research suggests that this additional time between parents and teachers benefits the relationship by being able to talk and share their ideas (Orellana, Monkman, and Macgillivray, 2002).

Training/ECT

My experience prior to working in mainstream relied so heavily on parental collaboration to function. While studying to become a teacher I was always amazed at how little of the training was directly related to building those successful relationships with parents. I was always wondering when the 'parent module' would come up. In truth, I don't feel it ever did. I was never fully sure what the school's expectations were when I first started in terms of meetings and protocols. This isn't something that is explicitly discussed, and I felt a bit silly asking. Again, going back to the question of time, when would SLT and mentors fit this in in the running of a school day? When would Early career teachers fit this in on top of their university course and their regular responsibilities? Additionally, if left to the school then training becomes more subjective, potentially leading to issues of modelling poor communication and standards. The new Early career framework (ECF) added significant amounts of paperwork to those involved. I always felt a pang of guilt when I walked past my mentor's classroom and found that they were staying late on another Zoom, completing paperwork and modules etc.

My peers and I completed our ECF with different providers and I was curious to know if anyone else felt as though they had been adequately trained in this area. It turned out that they all had the same feeling: that they had not been suitably trained to tackle situations with parents in an effective way. We joked about how ridiculous it is that we need to be trained to communicate effectively with other humans, but that's exactly what we needed. It wasn't as easy as just having a conversation on the street about the weather; there were so many things to think of and as ECTs we were busy worrying about Teacher Standards and School Policy and getting things right.

I remember feeling increasingly afraid of upsetting or offending a parent as I wasn't sure how to approach things like clean clothing, lost reading books, and incomplete homework, as well as children being significantly behind or struggling in their learning. I found myself unsure of policy more than anything else. I was always wondering: "Is this something I say to the parents or is this something the FLO or Principle should be discussing?"

There are a few points of interest here but in terms of parental engagement and ECTs, it's difficult to start off your career deliberately withholding the truth. It places all parties in such a vulnerable position. Unfortunately, I know this happens in many schools as there are simply more children with high needs and not enough staff/ training for staff. I have been the 1:1 who has been placed at a table to support other children, as well as the child whose needs have secured funding for my position. It always remained an area or topic that was never discussed.

> I'm worried about getting in trouble with the principal by saying something accidently to a parent when they ask about their child's progress, especially when it comes to the children with EHCPs. I also haven't really looked at their targets as much as I should. I am supposed to direct their 1:1 but sometimes feel like there is no time to talk about it and feel like neither of us know how to implement the targets. It's a lot on top of the rest that we are trying to get to grips with. I know they aren't making progress because their 1:1 is supporting a table of other children. The decision came from the SLT and I've been told by other staff that it's the same in their classrooms and that's the way it is, but that I shouldn't relay this to the parent. The SENCo is always so busy.
>
> ECT, London

A parent and staff member made the interesting point that there is insufficient information made available to staff that would help them support children and be better equipped to understand where they may need or qualify for more support. In terms of training for ECTs, medical diagnoses and SEND-related units of work also don't seem to be factored in, or focused on, to the degree needed when studying to achieve QTS.

> I am quite objective: the improvement in medicine means more children are surviving difficult births but social care and education provision isn't keeping up with that. Had my son, for example, been born 5 years earlier he wouldn't have survived but we don't have those conversations. Additionally, we are (in secondary) rarely made aware of those children who were very premature, their delay - even at 12+ - is significant!
>
> Parent #3 and Staff member in Education

Monthly meetings and weekly check-ins with parents could all prove to be effective in relaying any relevant information and provide ECTs with the opportunity to ask questions to SLTs and any external agencies. ECTs can begin to pick up the different terms used and get a better idea of what the parents are hoping to achieve or focus on.

> No one ever tells you any of these sorts of norms and do's and don'ts. When it comes to SEN we need more training to understand the parents and what goes on for them, but also support for us as ECTs to not carry it all on our own. Some of the children would have people come in and I never knew what they were there for so couldn't even inform parents or talk about it.
>
> ECT, Liverpool

In my experience, meetings with external agencies that occur more frequently and involve the parents produce better results and support engagement. I have been in a post where there were very few meetings, involving external agencies such as Occupational Therapists and Speech and language Therapists (SaLT) that I was able to attend. In contrast, I have been in posts where the beginning of the year saw the IEP process include a multidisciplinary approach whereby the Specialist, Lead Teacher, Teacher, OT, SLP, and Physical Education would all sit down together with the parents and discuss the upcoming IEP. This kept everyone on the same page but, most importantly, allowed the parents to be actively involved from the beginning and able to give their feedback.

Many of my peers were so completely overwhelmed with the range of support needs in their classroom, including those with EHCPs. My own 1:1 in my classroom was so wonderful and willing to learn. I was lucky enough to have the skills and experience from previous roles to provide them with high levels of support. I used my ECT time each week to work with them to ensure they were comfortable with the child's targets and to switch things up when progress was slow, and problem solve, and this was invaluable for both of us. It allowed me to oversee how the child was responding to certain programmes put in place and to check for ways we could improve our teaching to benefit the child. This, in turn, allowed the 1:1 to relay the outcomes and useful information to the parent at drop-off and pick-up times. Again, just keeping the parent in the loop, giving the information, and asking for the feedback.

Breakdowns in relationships

Interactions are not always easy. There are often uncomfortable conversations that must be had for both the parent and the staff. What's key is how these conversations are approached and subsequently followed up. Different schools have different procedures; in some schools the teachers are left to contact parents, while other schools may choose to have members of SLT make these difficult phone calls.

The following describes a situation faced by a new teacher. There had been an unravelling of the relationship between the parent and them as the child was displaying more challenging behaviours throughout the year. The child was unable to remain in the classroom, would unlock the door and bolt into the surrounding area of the school, climb out windows and shout insults at staff in front of peers. Often the class was evacuated, or another child had to go to the office with an SOS card if there wasn't enough staff. The situation worsened and the teacher often had to make phone calls home to inform the parents of what had happened. These phone calls often consisted of abusive language by the parents to the teacher.

The situation escalated. One afternoon the parent expressed that they believed the staff were bullying their child and insults were shouted to all of us in the corridor. Granted these comments and insults were not intentionally aimed at me, as I wasn't the child's teacher, but I just so happened to have come upon the situation and I shut the door to prevent any children from hearing. The child's teacher was called a range of vulgar insults and objects were thrown across the room. Raised voices and swear words continued as the parent moved outside to collect the child's sibling.

In a situation like this, where a child clearly had higher support needs to successfully and safely remain in school, we learnt that there was an obvious need for significant amounts of successful collaboration. However, after numerous instances of these types of episodes, how could the relationship have been repaired? Should that teacher have been expected to continue to speak to the parent following this incident? If the teacher had been an employee at a supermarket, security would have removed the individual and probably banned them from returning to the shop due to verbal assault. If they were a member of staff in a GP practice, this would not have been tolerated.

In this case they were required to interact following the situation until a new member of staff decided that this wasn't appropriate, and all interactions would occur through them. By this point, however, the damage had been done to both their relationship and the mental health of the staff.

As many who were asked about this element of engagement agreed that both staff and parents can often be tricky to deal with, how do we prevent this breakdown from occurring in the first case? What events usually lead up to this?

An opportunity to meet more frequently, when convenient for all parties, could lead to more successful conversations as parents are not always contacted for something negative. I also feel as though there should be more staff support in instances where parents conduct themselves in a manner that harms the relationship or wellbeing of staff. Setting a standard early on that any abusive language or behaviour will not be tolerated and will have consequences. Similarly, everyone working as a team to support each other when things do go sour is useful.

> There are good pastoral staff and there are weak ones. The ones that don't bother to make calls/contact are the ones that make things difficult for everyone.
>
> Previous Teacher #1 in both Mainstream/SEN settings, BESD school, SEN Further Education

Some of those I reached out to were able to answer as both a parent of a child with SEND and a member of staff within education. It was so wonderful to read comments from people who with their 'parent hat' on they could be honest in saying that sometimes staff are hard to work with, but who equally felt that when they put their 'staff hat' on that some parents can be difficult too.

> My own view is that those parents of children with SEN can be very tricky to deal with. Quite often they try to beat you with the paperwork and that will eventually lead to breakdowns in the relationship.
>
> Parent #3 and Staff member in Education

> I think parents and staff can be equally difficult to deal with, but there seems to be an element of 'them v. us' when breakdowns happen. When EHCPs or SEN are involved, I have found that this breakdown happens more frequently. Everyone is worried they are being blamed for lack of progress or something not done right.
>
> Staff, or at least the majority of them, are usually doing their best, but there are some that just don't know how to interact with parents at all and I think it creates a sour relationship and nothing is going to be achieved for the child this way. I tell staff to listen when parents tell them about their child as they know things we never will. Likewise, parents have a lot that goes on at home, but don't always understand what goes on for staff at school and have unrealistic expectations of what schools can physically do with what they have.
>
> I have often told friends who are pushing to send their child with moderate support needs to a mainstream school, to go with an SEN school. They will have more provision as the budget and set up of the school allows it!
>
> I'm a parent and a SENCo so when my child's teacher forgets something I always give the benefit of the doubt because I have been there! They are not just responsible for my child but usually 30 others. I think this is forgotten about and I think some parents are definitely just in it for the moan.
>
> Huddersfield, SENCo

Some parents felt that staff at mainstream schools just didn't understand their child's needs and only really seemed to give them time if they had an EHCP. They felt that SEN settings seemed to handle difficult conversations in a better way, and they didn't feel as though there was a threat of exclusion looming at the end of any phone call.

> My child was always in trouble in their mainstream school. I always felt really scared that he would be excluded from school and I wouldn't be able to get him in another. School were always just telling me how bad things were and what he had done but I was never given anything good or offered any solutions. We made

> the decision to move him to an SEN and it just seemed to make everything stop. I think that he just needed the right fit and maybe the other school didn't have the expertise or the skills that he needed. I think they didn't know how to handle his frustrations. He found it hard to communicate all the time and they worked on that at his new school. I would advise parents to stop worrying so much about what it looks like to go to an SEN school, it was the best thing we ever did for him and us!
>
> Parent of child with SEN

EHCP

For many, the road to a diagnosis is the hope that it will open more doors in terms of support provided to the family.

> We were so thankful to have gotten our daughter diagnosed because she was falling so far behind across her learning and we were trying for years, then COVID happened and we thought it was never going to happen. The diagnosis let us apply and she got her high needs funding and has support at school. I know parents always talk about it like it's a golden ticket, but it really does just feel like their education is secured or guaranteed.
>
> Parent of child with SEN in mainstream

> My son is in a SEN school. Over the last few years (maybe since his EHCP has become a legal obligation) the school has become more "distant"; the cosy friendliness has disappeared. As always, as a professional and a parent, it's those who shout loudest who get most support, and if you work the availability of support is poorer - especially financially.
>
> Parent #3 and Staff member in Education

> When the EHCP was introduced, "legal document" was bandied around so much that it's bound to make practitioners paranoid about meeting needs!! So much seems to be down to the LA too: my son's provision is from Gloucestershire and I cannot fault them! Yes, we're a huge county and there are delays when staff leave/transfer but they are on it as best they can be.
>
> Parent #3 and Staff member in Education

> We have had children with an EHCP and honestly weren't able to meet their needs as well as the local SEN school could have, but I think parents still have a stigma attached to it. I worry that if we are honest with them that they will feel we are trying to get rid of their child when really, we are just trying to advocate for the child. I had a parent threaten me when I suggested her son would be better placed in a school that had hoists in the bathroom and trained staff. Her son was great, but we didn't have the resources and we lost two-thirds members of staff just to facilitate the bathroom and it took away any chance of independence for the child.
>
> Principal, Leeds

Conclusion

The collaborative relationship between home and school is a topic that extends across the world. It always generates interest as we seek new ways to improve existing practice and to disseminate our efforts when they are working for us. Many wonderful articles exist that explore this dynamic relationship from around the world (Garvis et al., 2021), but there has not been that focus towards SEN in the same capacity. It's important for both staff and parents to be aware of the barriers from each other's perspective. As there are so many additional barriers facing those parents of children with SEN, at the very least being aware of them is a small step in the right direction to facilitate successful engagement.

What is working?

- Regular communication of any kind from all professionals in school – Senior leaders, teachers, admin, Family Liaison Officer.
- Regular parent phone calls to deliver more complex or difficult messages.
- Home school contact book with key informal messages.
- "In touch" system to send anything from text reminders to formal letters, to consultations.
- Feedback that's acted on – they felt listened to and that was appreciated.
- Supporting parents with school-related information they may find difficult to process such as sorting out canteen accounts. But also supporting them with non-school-related processes such as applying for DLA/PIP/Transport arrangements. They really appreciate the support in navigating some of the more complex systems they have to work with when they have a child with SEN.
- Praise postcards so they know when their child has particularly succeeded.
- Recently launched a whole-week transition which then had a chance for the new Year 6 parents to come and meet the teacher and see the work the students had done.
- Not overloading SEN students and their parents with homework, but just choosing a few key pieces.
- Explaining clearly (in language that isn't too "educationally professional jargon") what is going well for the student and what they are struggling with and how parents can assist – both academically and pastorally.

Lead of specialist provision for students with profound, severe and complex learning needs

References

BASW. (2018). *Empty Promises: The crisis in supporting children with SEND.* Accessed 22th August 2022. [online] www.basw.co.uk. https://www.basw.co.uk/resources/empty-promises-crisis-supporting-children-send

DePape, A.-M. and Lindsay, S. (2014). Parents' experiences of caring for a child with autism spectrum disorder. *Qualitative Health Research*, 25(4), pp. 569–583. doi:10.1177/1049732 314552455.

Garvis, S., Phillipson, S., Harju-Luukkainen, H. and Sadownik, A.R. (2021). *Parental Engagement and Early Childhood Education Around the World.* London: Routledge. doi:10.4324/9780367823917.

Jigyel, K., Miller, J.A., Mavropoulou, S. and Berman, J. (2019). Parental involvement in supporting their children with special educational needs at school and home in Bhutan. *Australasian Journal of Special and Inclusive Education*, [online] 43(01), pp. 54–68. doi:10.1017/jsi.2019.3.

Lamb, B. (2019). Statutory assessment for special educational needs and the warnock report; the first 40 years. *Frontiers in Education*, [online] 4. doi:10.3389/feduc.2019.00051.

Lendrum, A., Barlow, A. and Humphrey, N. (2013). Developing positive school-home relationships through structured conversations with parents of learners with special educational needs and disabilities (SEND). doi:10.1111/1471-3802.12023.

MacCormack, J., FitzGerald, C., Whitley, J. and Sider, S. (2022). Lessons learned: Home-school collaboration for students with SEN during emergency remote teaching. *Leadership and Policy in Schools*, pp. 1–18. doi:10.1080/15700763.2022.2081217.

O'Connor, U., Bates, J., Finlay, J. and Campbell, A. (2021). Parental involvement during COVID-19: Experiences from the special school. *European Journal of Special Needs Education*, pp. 1–14. doi:10.1080/08856257.2021.1967297.

Orellana, M.F., Monkman, K. and MacGillivray, L. (2002). *Parents and Teachers Talk about Literacy Success. CIERA Report.* Accessed 26th August 2022. [online] Ed.gov. https://eric.ed.gov/?id=ED468905

Parentkind. (2021). *Parent Voice Report 2021.* Accessed 22th August 2022. [online] https://www.parentkind.org.uk/research-and-policy/parent-research/annual-parent-voice-reports/parent-voice-report-2021

Prince, A.M.T., Hodge, J., Bridges, W.C. and Katsiyannis, A. (2017). Predictors of postschool education/training and employment outcomes for youth with disabilities. *Career Development and Transition for Exceptional Individuals*, [online] 41(2), pp. 77–87. doi:10.1177/2165143417698122.

Rattenborg, K., MacPhee, D., Walker, A.K. and Miller-Heyl, J. (2018). Pathways to parental engagement: Contributions of parents, teachers, and schools in cultural context. *Early Education and Development*, 30(3), pp. 315–336. doi:10.1080/10409289.2018.1526577.

Robbins, J. and Dempster, K. (2021). *The Four Pillars of Parental Engagement: Empowering Schools to Connect Better with Parents and Pupils.* Bancyfelin, Carmarthen, Wales: Independent Thinking Press.

Scorgie, K. and Sobsey, D. (2017). So you think we can trust? (Re)building home-school collaboration with families of children with disability. *International Perspectives on Inclusive Education*, pp. 255–271. doi:10.1108/s1479-363620170000010026.

Spear, S., Spotswood, F., Goodall, J. and Warren, S. (2021). Reimagining parental engagement in special schools – a practice theoretical approach. *Educational Review*, 74, p. 7. doi: 10.1080/00131911.2021.1874307

Stefanidis, A., King-Sears, M.E. and Kyriakidou, N. (2021). School bells are ringing, but can parents attend? Responses from employed parents of children with SEND. *Community, Work & Family*, pp.1–20. doi:10.1080/13668803.2021.1984210.

Warnock, M. (1978). Children with special needs: the Warnock Report. *BMJ*, 1(6164), pp. 667–668. doi:10.1136/bmj.1.6164.667.

Warnock, M. (2005). Special Schools or not? *Education Review*, [online] 19(1). Accessed 13th August 2022. https://educationpublishing.com/wp-content/uploads/2019/06/Education_Review_Vol.19_No.1.pdf#page=18

7 Reflections

Throughout this book, the thread of each segment linked to parental engagement has looked at literature, strategies, frameworks and real-life experiences. The many wonderful and insightful contributors featured within the book, and the shared passion they had around successful outcomes for children and their families, focussed on the following areas;

- Parent Councils
- Engaging with the disengaged
- Special Educational Needs
- Voluntary action
- Wellbeing and mental health
- Strengthening links
- School–home experiences of collaboration in various form

Discussion around school cultures and parental collaboration is by no means a new initiative. However, the purpose of this book is to create an opportunity for educational professionals to consider their current approach and enable conversations to develop around new initiatives, based on the lived experiences of others.

Schools have developed a similar narrative to one another, with mirrored opportunities for families to engage. However, as society and the needs of our families change, the approach to working with families must also be continuously reviewed.

Understanding how best to complete this connection and generate successful outcomes as a result, can seem overwhelming initially – however, it can and will be achieved if we allow it. The attempts by the parent council at St Nicholas Primary School and Flakefeet Primary Schools hit record are prime examples of that.

The intention of sharing the tried, tested and Ofsted approved results (please see Chapter 1), is to encourage other schools to try the same approach. My passion for successful inclusive and collaborative approaches stems from the belief that we are stronger together.

To embed a 'whole-family approach to education' and a 'whole-school approach to engagement' would be to strengthen our schools, the education system and our communities immensely.

The closure of Sure Start Children Centres is a heart-breaking and concerning movement. This pivotal first stage of interaction can pave the way for families to engage with others. Without it, when do we start to open the lines of communication? Especially when we consider the most vital stages in a child's life is from birth to 5 years. I am, in equal measure, concerned about the needs of our families, and excited about the possibilities available to ensure that we can make to improve children's outcomes.

Working within a school is an honour and for those of us working within education, we have the opportunity to provide a vital link with families. Whether that be through;

- Forest School Toddler Groups
- Parent Councils
- Music and number 1 hits
- Interlinking settings and educational communities
- SEN provisions
- Parent, Teacher and Friends Association (PTFA)
- Working with staff to review, reflect and rewrite your school's current parent policy
- Working through challenging circumstances – e.g. pandemics
- Developing new opportunities within teacher training
- Reflecting on collaborative approaches with families that have English as an additional language (EAL)
- Improving the way in which transitions are conducted at any stage of a child's education
- Reading and reflecting on the blueprint by ParentKind for parent-friendly schools
- Developing relationship approaches, from nursery to secondary, and every stage in-between
- Creating safe spaces for positive conversations
- Maintaining and developing healthy relationships

The future

The Schools White Paper (DfE, 2010) identified that schools will increasingly be accountable to parents for the progress and achievement of their pupils. Along with the increase of recognition that schools have on involving parents in their children's learning (DfE, 2010).

Whilst many understand the impact of parental engagement, the ongoing discussion around how best to achieve it, highlights that there is a missing link between identification and successful outcomes. Impactful documents, such as the Plowden Report (1967), concluded that parental attitudes towards children's schooling was a bigger contributor to their child's success than the school itself or home circumstances.

The obligation for equality between home and school is essential for success: 'this does not mean professionals dictating the terms of the relationship but rather a more equal approach based on respect, trust, empathy and integrity' (Pugh, 2010). A subjective recommendation for research moving forward would be to identify the best ways of implementing and delivering interventions to meet the needs of their families, further highlighting the need for schools to become 'community centres', similar to the experience provided for by Children Centre's. For intervention groups, such as curriculum sessions, the advantage of cognitive psychology would play a key factor: 'it is known to improve long-term retention and thus have clear implications for educational settings' (Carpenter, Cepeda, Rohrer, Kang, and Pashler, 2012).

The most impressive and successful programmes have been those that have included family learning: 'parent's take their place alongside educators in the schooling of their children, fitting together their knowledge of children, teaching, and learning with teacher's knowledge' (Pushor and Ruitenberg, 2005). Breaking the mould of home and school being separate entities and moving towards an equally balanced approach, would enable interactions to be proactive, rather than reactive. For this to be achieved successfully, communication needs to be two-way, genuine, frequent and meaningful. Families need the opportunity to grow with the school, and schools require the opportunity to enable this powerful force to not only establish itself with the fundamental building blocks of their school ethos, but also be given the correct tools to flourish. Providing robust coverage within teacher training programmes and structured blueprints for successful collaborations will enable schools to achieve a regenerated approach – providing invaluable support to the children, families, staff and communities that they serve.

References

Carpenter, S.K., Cepeda, N.J., Rohrer, D., Kang, S.H.K. and Pashler, H. (2012). Using spacing to enhance diverse forms of learning: Review of recent research and implications for instruction. *Educational Psychology Review*, 24, pp. 369–378. doi: 10.1007/s10648-012-9205-z

Central Advisory Council for Education. (1967). *The Plowden Report, Children and Their Primary Schools*. London: HMSO.

Department for Education (DfE). (2010). The importance of teaching: The schools white Paper 2010. https://assets.publishing.service.gov.uk/government/uploads/system/uploads/attachment_data/file/175429/CM-7980.pdf

Pugh, G. (2010). Improving outcomes for young children: How can we narrow the gap? *Early Years*, 30(1), pp. 5–14.

Pushor, D. and Ruitenberg, C.W. (2005). Parent engagement and leadership teaching and learning research exchange. https://www.researchgate.net/publication/326752113_PARENT_ENGAGEMENT_AND_LEADERSHIP_TEACHING_AND_LEARNING_RESEARCH_EXCHANGE

Index

Pages in *italics* refer to figures.

Adams, K.S. 102
Armstrong, Paul 47
Atkins, Sue 71–72
augmentative and alternative communication device (AAC) 117

blueprint for parent-friendly schools 47–48
Board-Certified Behavior Analyst (BCBA) 113, 117
Body, A. 3, 80–93
Bourdieu, P. 104
Bower, V. 53
Bryk, A.S. 102

Canterbury Christ Church University 21, 109
'capital' and 'habitus' 104
Caplan, J.G. 107
Chatter Box 61–62
children: during lockdown 99; outcomes for 131; with SEN needs 55
The Children's Act of 2004 46
Children's Centre 1, 108, 131–132
Christenson, S.L. 102
Clarke, Lorna 8–10
Cobb, W. 52–54, 69–71
collaboration 3, 8, 18; community and communication 46–47; home and school 47–48; inclusive practice and 49; leadership and structures 54–56
collaborative policy 52
communication 1; ambiverts 29; be curious 44; building healthy communication mindset *see* healthy communication mindset; and collaboration 56; community and 46; introverts and extroverts 29–30; managing during crisis 41; positively under pressure 40–42
confidence 10, 13, 21, 32, 43–44, 53, 55, 60, 104

connection building: be inclusive 43; be in moment 43–44; communication with confidence 43; connections everywhere 44; empathy and kindness 43
The Conventions on the Rights of the Child 52
cost 28, 75, 77–78, 81–82, 88–90, 94
council members 6–8, 13–21, 109–110
Covey, Stephen 33
COVID-19 pandemic 10–11, 25, 34, 54, 71, 81, 86, 98–99
culture of philanthropy 90–92

Dempsey, Bethany 57–58
Dempster, K. 3, 24–45
Department for Education (DfE) 8, 10, 81
DISC color preferences 33, 35–36
Disclosure and Barring Service (DBS) 89
Dominance, Influence, Steadiness and Conscientiousness (DISC) 29–30, 33, 38, 65–36
donors 84, 91–92

early career framework (ECF) 124
Early Years Foundation Stage (EYFS) 57, 61
Early Years Pupil Premium (EYPP) 56
educational establishments 3, 104–106
educational setting 1, 48, 54, 56, 95, 132
Education Endowment Foundation 66, 94
education, health and care plan (EHCP) 4, 66–67, 113, 121, 123–125, 127–129
empathy 27–28, 34–35, 37, 39, 43, 69, 132
'Engaging Parents in Raising Achievement: Do Parents Know They Matter?' 94
engaging with disengaged 131; barriers to engagement 95; Kirsten Terry : engaging with disengaged families 96–98
English as an additional language (EAL) 51–52, 70, 132
Epstein, J.L. 104, 108
Equality Act 2010 28

Facebook 9–10, 76
family learning 132
Family Liaison Officer (FLO) 51, 65, 72, 74, 97, 123–124, 129
fear of public speaking/'Glossophobia' 31
fear rejection 24, 26
filters 34, 43
Flakefeet Primary Schools 131
Forest School Toddler group 73–75, 132
Frost, Claire 60–62
Fry, Stephen 77
fundraising: challenges in 84–85; increase in donated income 83–84; in schools 82–83

Gisewhite, R. 102
Goodall, J. 94, 115
Good Morning Britain and *The One Show* 77
governors 5, 16, 41, 48, 86, 88, 98, 107
Griffiths, Lucy 72–73
GROW model 36

Hargreaves, K. 102
Harris, A. 94
The Head of School 9
Headteacher 6, 9, 13, 17
healthy communication mindset: building strong connections *see* connection building; building trust with different types of people 38–40, *39*; creating safe space for positive conversations 37; developing a growth mindset 30–31; DISC colours to listen effectively 35; listen fully 32; listening virtually 34–35; making listening visible 33; managing difficult conversations 35–37; managing your personal energy 42–43; overcome anxiety/personal challenges 31–32; positive communication under pressure 40–42; stay in moment 34; understanding 33–34
home links and COVID-19 71–73
home schooling/home learning 71–72
Hornby, G. 104
How to Survive in Teaching 26
Hull, D.M. 104

individual education plans (IEPs) 113
Institute for Fiscal Studies (IFS) 25, 81

James, C. 49
Johnson, U.Y. 104

Kell, E. 26
Key Instant Recall Facts (KIRFs) 11
Kim, Y. 108
Knoff, H.M. 107

Lafaele, R. 104
Lamb, B. 66
Language Learning and Intercultural Understanding in the Primary School 53
Lau, E. 75–76
Leeds Beckett University 26
Lee, Hannah 10–11
Longman, Kerry 63–65

The Manchester Transition project 10
Man, Nicki 54–56
Marsh Academy Community Hub (MACH) 67
Martin, Chris 103
Maslow's Hierarchy of needs 24, *24*, *39*, 39–40, 50–51, *51*
McClenaghan, Catherine 113–129
McNeal, R.B. 104
McPartlin, Dave 76–78
mental health and wellbeing 3, 98; Alex Wallace: reflective practice as professional 99–101
Menu of Learning Opportunities (MoLO) 69–70
Moss, P. 107
multi-agency working 48, 59

National College for Teaching and Leadership (2014) 54
The National Council for Voluntary Organisations (NCVO) 15
National Curriculum 68
National Funding Formula 82
National Lottery Fund 83
National Statistics 56
Neuro Leadership Institute 37
1997 White Paper, England 106
nursery 56–61, 108, 132

Oak Academy 56
Ofsted 2–3, 18, 21–22, 41, 48, 99, 131
Outdoor Play and Learning (OPAL) school 60

parental collaboration 4, 10, 123, 131
parental engagement 3; according to staff 118–119; barriers 102, *103*, 122; breakdown in relationships 125–128; Chris Martin: effective partnerships of parents and schools 103–105; collaborative movement *105*, 105–106; communication 117–118; during COVID-19 115; EHCP 128–129; family and school 115; involvement 115–117; lack of money 122–123; between mainstream and SEN settings 119–122; overcoming barriers 106–107; parent councils 107–109; SEN 114–115; St Nicholas Parent Council 109–110; time 123; training 123–125

Index

parent council (PC) 2–3, 48, 59, 131–132; 5-step vision plan 6; aim of 13; awards and success 21; celebrating 15; collaborative approach 6, 7, 20–21; communication 13–14; conversations and opportunities 15–16; council members 6; definition 5; final reflection 22; good communication 7; group of parents 13; Hannah Lee: collaborating with parent council 10–11; impact in school 10; Lorna Clarke: setting up new Council prior to Covid 8–10; managing volunteers 14–15; Ofsted 21–22; personable approach for parents 8; PTFAs and 11–12, *12*; recruiting 7; role 14; setting 5; vision 5

parent council policy 17, *18*; 'Code of Conduct' 16; confidentiality 17; council meetings 18; outcomes for children 19; planning and building 18; projects 18–19; roles and responsibilities 16–17; volunteer policy 17

parentkind 47–48, 75, 109, 132

parent power 78

Parent, Teacher and Friends Association (PTFA) 11, *12*, 73, 75–76, 132

Parent Teacher Association (PTA) 80, 82–83, 90, 92

Pathological Demand Avoidance (PDA) 57

personal energy 30, 42–43

personality 26, 29, 37–38

personal wellbeing 25, 43

Petrie, P. 107

philanthropy 3, 15, 90–92

picture exchange communication system (PECs) 113

Poland, G. 107

PoPA group/team 109–110

positive mindset 36, 42

positive relationships 3; building with other people 28–29; connection and 25; and healthy communication *see* healthy communication mindset; trusted relationships 26; way of building 26–28

primary schools 59–62, 74, 80–82, 86, 90, 93

professionals experiences and top tips: Bethany Dempsey–working with parents and support 57–58; Claire Frost: transition approach 60–62; Dave McPartlin–sense of belonging and community 76–78; Emily Lau: areas of success and opportunities 75–76; Emma Read: working with families and children 66–68; Forest School Toddler group 73–75; Heather Woodcock: successful collaborative working 49–51, *51*; Kerry Longman: transitions from primary to secondary 63–65; Lucy Griffiths: communication with parents 72–73; Nicki Man: leading a school during COVID-19 54–56; Niomi Clyde Roberts: working with families within primary setting 59–60; Sue Atkins: parenting 71–72; Wendy Cobb: EAL–cultural identities and family traditions 52–54; Wendy Cobb: trainee teachers completing their training 69–71

Provision Evaluation officers (PEOs) 68

Quality First teaching (QFT) 68

Raffaele, L.M. 107
Read, Emma 66–68
relational trust 102
reputation 18, 28, 41
Robbins, J. 3, 24–45
Roberts, Niomi Clyde 59–60
Rock, David 37
Roffey Park Institute *27, 39*

Schneider, B.L. 102
School Centred Initial Teacher Training course 69
schools: added nicety 85; community 8, 21, 80, 82, 87; council 6, 19–20, 22, 98; cultures 131; engagement of volunteers *see* volunteers; fundraising in 82–83; ideologically for fundraising 85; ideologically opposed 85; initiatives 4; and settings 3; survival 85; voluntary action efforts *see* voluntary action in education; working within education 132
school's senior leadership team (SLT) 6, 26, 72
The Schools White Paper 132
secondary schools 62–65
SEND Code of Practice 65–66
SENDCOs 51, 66–67, 119, 122
Senior Leadership Team (SLT) 6, 8–9, 13, 16–17
SEN provisions 66, 132
Sheffield's Voluntary Sector Studies Network 109
'social enterprise'-type activities 83
social media 41, 56, 69, 75–78
Spear, S. 115
Special Educational Needs (SEN) 66–68, 131; department 67; in mainstream schools 113–114; parental engagement 114–115; schools 3–4; teamwork 67; transition process 66
special educational needs and disability (SEND) 50, 66, 68, 96, 113, 122, 124, 127
Special Educational Needs Co-ordinator (SENCo) 1, 62–63
Spotswood, F. 115
Statutory Inspection of Anglican Methodist Schools (SIAMS) 109
Stewart, E.B. 105

St Nicholas Primary School 10–11, 13, 15, 21, 131
Summer School 64–65
Sure Start Children Centres 108, 131
Survey Monkey 21

Teachwire.net in 2017 26
Terry, Kirsten 96–98
trainee teacher programmes 68–71
trusted relationships: based on Wheel of Trust 39, 39–40; *see also* Maslow's hierarchy of needs; building 25; communication 25
2018 Teacher Well-Being Index 26
2021 Teacher Wellbeing Index 25

voluntary action in education 3, 131; to achieve success *see* voluntary action success; groups 107; school community 80; schools attraction 81–82; as a 'wicked problem' 90–91
voluntary action success: creating a philanthropic narrative 92; identifying dual benefits 92; investing in people and skills 92; proactive approach 91–92
Voluntary Sector Studies Network (VSSN) 21, 109
volunteers: benefits of 86; challenges in engaging 88–89; as free resource 88; as links to community 87; massive cost 90; role models and support for children 87; successfully engaging 88; as support for teachers 87; volunteers activities 86

Wallace, Alex 99–101
Wall, D. 102
Warnock, M. 113
Warren, S. 115
wellbeing: Maslow's hierarchy of needs 24, *24*; and mental health 98–101, 131; teacher 25–26; through positive relationships *see* healthy communication mindset
WhatsApp 9, 15
Woodcock, Heather 49–51, *51*

For Product Safety Concerns and Information please contact our EU representative GPSR@taylorandfrancis.com
Taylor & Francis Verlag GmbH, Kaufingerstraße 24, 80331 München, Germany

www.ingramcontent.com/pod-product-compliance
Lightning Source LLC
Chambersburg PA
CBHW080613230426
43664CB00019B/2879